COMBAT LEGEND

B-24
LIBERATOR

Martin Bowman

Airlife

Copyright © 2003 Airlife Publishing Ltd

First published in the UK in 2003
by Airlife Publishing Ltd

Text written by Martin W. Bowman
Profile illustrations drawn by Dave Windle
Cover painting by Jim Brown – The Art of Aviation Co. Ltd

British Library Cataloguing-in-Publication Data
    A catalogue record for this book
    is available from the British Library

ISBN 1 84037 403 9

Printed in China

For a complete list of all Airlife titles please contact:

Airlife Publishing Ltd
101 Longden Road, Shrewsbury, SY3 9EB, England
E-mail: sales@airlifebooks.com
Website: www.airlifebooks.com

Contents

Liberator Timeline

1939

20 January — Preliminary specifications of the Model 32 ready and construction begins.

29 December — XB-24 made its maiden flight.

1940

June — France places contract for 175 LB-30MFs – order taken over by the British after the fall of France.

1941

February — Manufacturing pool to build B-24 Liberators officially established. Construction of a fourth Liberator production line by the US Government for the Ford Motor Company begins at Willow Run, Dearborn, Michigan.

16 June — First of 9 B-24As accepted by the Army Air Corps.

September — Two B-24As take part in the Harriman mission to Moscow. One continues via the Middle East, India, Australia and Hawaii. The other returns to the USA via Egypt, central Africa, the South Atlantic and Brazil.

7 December — Japanese attack on Pearl Harbor.

11 December — Germany declares war on the USA.

1942

— Second Liberator production line at Consolidated-Vultee, Fort Worth, Texas, opens.

17 January — 7th BG in Java fly the first AAF Liberator combat sorties.

23 January — First B-24D delivered.

12 February — 10th AF activated for combat in the CBI theatre.

23 February — First 8th AF echelons arrive in England.

11 June — 11th AF bombers make first attack on Kiska, main Japanese air base in the Aleutians.

12 June — US heavy bombers bomb a European target for the first time. Thirteen B-24Ds commanded by Col Harry H. Halverson, part of the HALPRO force *en route* to join the 10th AF to bomb Tokyo from the Chinese mainland, use their staging base at Fayid on the Great Bitter Lake, near the Suez Canal, to attack the oil fields at Ploesti, Romania.

Aug–September — Allied Air Forces, SWPA, renamed 5th AF, help repulse Japanese thrusts at Buna in New Guinea. Operations feature airlift of troops into and within the theatre.

9 October — 93rd BG of the 8th Air Force flies its maiden mission, to the Fives-Lille steelworks in Belgium – the first mission flown from East Anglia in which over 100 bombers participate.

October — US aircraft in the Pacific start sowing mines in narrow waters, river mouths and harbours in the Malay Peninsula, Japanese-occupied areas of the south-west Pacific and the China coast, and in the inland seas around Japan itself.

8 November — Operation *Torch*: invasion of North Africa. US 12th AF take part.

1943

23 January — Beginning of the Combined Bomber offensive in Europe by the AAF and RAF Bomber Command.

27 January — First AAF attack on Germany (U-boat construction yards at Wilhelmshaven); 91 B-24s and B-17s dispatched.

March — Consolidated and Vultee companies merge and later become Convair. Third production line operated by Douglas Aircraft started at Tulsa, Oklahoma. North American at Dallas, Texas begins operation of the fifth and final major Liberator plant.

13 May — Axis surrender in North Africa.

10 July — Allied invasion of Sicily.

17 July — A record 322 8th AF bombers are dispatched to Hanover.

24 July — 'Blitz Week' costs the 8th AF about 100 aircraft and 90 combat crews, which leaves fewer than 200 heavy bombers ready for combat.

1 August — Operation *Tidal Wave* – raid on Romanian oil refinery at Ploesti by 177 B-24Ds from five groups: 44th, 93rd, 389th of the 8th AF, and the 98th and 376th BGs, 9th BC.

13 August — First raid on Balikpapan oilfields by B-24s of the 380th BG in a 17-hour sortie from Darwin, Australia.

August — AAF transfers all its B-24-equipped anti-submarine squadrons to the USN. Anti-Submarine Command disbanded.

9 September — Allied invasion of Italy. Italy surrenders.

1 October — 15th AF begins strategic bombing of German and Austrian targets from Italy.

2 November — Devastating US raid on Japanese main base at Rabaul.

1944

1 January — Establishment of US Strategic Air Forces in Europe Command to control operations of 8th and 15th AFs.

19–26 February — 'Big Week' series of sustained raids on German aircraft industry. Total losses amount to 226 US bombers.

Spring — 7th and 13th AFs concentrate on Japanese bases in eastern Caroline Islands, Truk and Ponape.

4-6 March — First Berlin raids.

March–June — Interdiction campaign to isolate north-west France, the area of Operation *Overlord*.

March–May — Operation *Strangle*: interdiction campaign to choke off German rail supply in Italy.

6 June — Operation *Overlord*, the invasion of north-west France: 2,362 bomber sorties involving 1,729 B-17s and B-24s are flown on D-Day, dropping 3,596 tons of bombs.

7 August — 492nd BG, 8th Air Force withdrawn from combat after losing 54 B-24s May–July 1944.

September — Peak inventory of 6,043 Liberators on operational strength worldwide, equipping 45 groups.

10 October — FEAF B-24s strike former Dutch oil refinery at Balikpapan, Borneo.

25 October — Invasion of Leyte: return to the Philippines.

1945

January — Allied air forces help defeat German forces engaged in the Battle of the Bulge.

February — Raids on Berlin: bombing offensive continues through to the last days of the war. In the Pacific, 7th AF bombers support US Marines on Iwo Jima.

13–15 February — 8th AF and RAF Bomber Command raze German city of Dresden. HE and firestorms cause 35,000 civilian deaths.

25 April — In its last mission of the war, B-24s of the 2nd Air Division, 8th AF, bomb four rail complexes at Berchtesgaden.

6 May — Victory in Italy Day announced.

7 May — German representatives surrender in the west.

6 August — First atomic bomb drop, on Hiroshima, Japan.

9 August — Second atomic bomb dropped on Nagasaki.

13 August — 11th Air Force flies its last mission of the war with a raid on Parasmishiro in the Kuriles.

14 August — Japanese Government surrenders.

30 September — As demobilisation begins, USAAF has 1,992,960 personnel (310,443 officers, 1,682,517 EM) in service. Peak strength was in March 1944, when total was 2,411,294 men.)

1. America's Liberator: Development History

Early in 1939 the US Army Air Corps (USAAC) drew up a requirement for a heavy bomber of better performance than the B-17, then in production. Chiefs of Staff were looking for a bomber with a greatly improved range of some 3,000 miles, with a top speed in excess of 300 mph and a ceiling of 35,000 ft. The Consolidated Company of San Diego, California had already completed a series of design studies into such a bomber. Chief architect was Isaac Machlin 'Mac' Laddon, who had joined the company in 1927 as chief engineer. Consolidated had a long history in building flying boats and a lengthy history in long-range aircraft design, many of the types owing their origins to Laddon.

When in May 1938 the French Government issued a specification to Consolidated for a heavy bomber, the company's early study was designated LB-30, for land-bomber. It was a landplane version of the Model 29 flying boat (PB2-Y). In June 1940 France placed a contract for 175 LB-30MFs (Mission Français) but the country was on the brink of defeat by the Nazis and the order was later taken over by Britain. Interest in the design was shown by the Army Air Corps (AAC) and it prompted a further design study, designated XB-24. Notably, this featured David R. Davis's high aspect ratio, low-drag, wing and the twin-finned empennage used on the Model 31 flying boat (P4Y-1).

By 20 January 1939, the preliminary specifications of the Model 32 were ready and construction started. It was to be powered by four Pratt & Whitney R-1830-33 Twin Wasp engines each capable of 1,200 hp on take-off and 1,000 hp at 14,500 ft. In February a wind tunnel test proved successful. Consolidated designers went to Wright Field to discuss their design with senior Air Corps officers, who suggested almost 30 changes to the preliminary specifications. A contract for a prototype was signed on 30 March 1939.

Innovative design

Aircraft like the Model 32 had never been conceived before and to turn this innovative design into a production aircraft would be extremely costly. It was of conventional structure, but among its more unusual features was a tricycle landing gear, the first to be fitted to a four-engined bomber. This would permit faster landings and take-offs. It had the added benefit of allowing for a heavier wing loading on the Davis aerofoil. The main landing gears were housed in the wing and they had to be long enough to clear the high bomb bays. The gears would be retracted outwards by electric motors. Bombs could be stowed vertically in the two halves of the bomb bay, thus enabling eight 1,100-lb bombs to be carried – twice the load of the B-17.

A catwalk connecting the flight deck and the tail section separated the bomb bay itself, which was enclosed by roller-shutter doors. A bombardier's enclosure was created in the nose of the deep fuselage, with a nose-socket fitted for a machine-gun. Behind the twin rudders was a tail gun position. Three 0.50-calibre guns and four 0.30-calibre Browning hand-operated

39-680, the XB-24 prototype, which flew for the first time on 29 December 1939. This photo was taken later, after the installation of armour plate and self-sealing tanks and relocation of the pitot tubes from the wings to the nose. It had also been re-engined with R-1830-41s in place of the earlier unsupercharged R-1830-33s. Convair retained 39-680 as a trials aircraft and company service aircraft. *(USAF)*

machine-guns were designed to be fired through openings in the fuselage sides and from nose, dorsal, and ventral positions.

On 27 April 1939 the AAC placed an initial contract for seven YB-24s for service trials in the autumn. These aircraft were similar to the XB-24 prototype, but the wing leading-edge slots were deleted and de-icing boots were fitted to the wings and tail. On 10 August 1939 a further order was received for 36 B-24A production models. Only nine aircraft were completed to B-24A standard, which were armed with 0.5-in machine-guns in the tail-gun position in place of the 0.30-in guns of earlier models. Experience gained by the RAF in Europe in other combat types led to the XB-24 receiving self-sealing fuel tanks and armour plate. Provision was made for seven crew.

B-24 takes to the air

On 26 October 1939 the Davis wing was married to the fuselage for the first time. On 29 December the XB-24 made its maiden flight from the Lindbergh Field at the Consolidated plant in San Diego, with William A. Wheatley at the controls. Wheatley was to lose his life on 2 June 1941, during the final acceptance flight of the Liberator Mk II for the RAF when a loose bolt jammed the elevator controls and the aircraft crashed.

The prototype's speed of 273 mph was 38 mph less than that estimated in the original specification, but more power could be achieved with turbo-supercharged engines in place of the mechanically supercharged 33s. On 26 July 1940 the AAC ordered that turbo-superchargers and leak-proof fuel tanks be installed. The bomber was redesignated XB-24B, with R-1830-41 Wasps giving 1,200 hp at 25,000 ft, and the wing slots were deleted. The improved prototype was flown on 1 February 1941.

The substitution was marked with the relocation of the oil coolers on each side of the radial engines instead of underneath, and this produced the characteristic elliptical cowling seen on all subsequent models. The aircraft underwent further cosmetic changes with the installation of a Martin A-3 dorsal turret and a Consolidated-built tail turret. A further nine of the 1940 consignment of 36 were completed in 1941 as B-24Cs.

A contest held at the Consolidated plant to select a name for the new bomber led to Dorothy Fleet, wife of the company's founder, the aviation pioneer Reuben H. Fleet, submitting the name 'Liberator'. She did so anonymously; it was selected and adopted even though John W. Thompson, Consolidated's public relations officer, tried to change the name to 'Eagle' in April 1942.

Nine B-24As, powered by R-1830-33 Wasps, were accepted by the AAC between 16 June and 10 July 1941. Though mounts for six 0.50- and two 0.30-calibre machine-guns were fitted,

B-24Ds for the AAF and the Anti-Submarine Groups under construction at the Convair plant at Fort Worth, Texas, in June 1943. More than 3,000 B-24s and C-87 cargo versions were built at the plant. (*General Dynamics*)

these aircraft went to the newly formed Air Corps Ferrying Command, which retained only a tail gun. Ferry Command's commanding officer was Col Robert Olds, and its *raison d'être* was to deliver aircraft to Montreal for ferrying to Britain. Olds also had broader powers to 'maintain such special air ferry service as may be required'. The first pilots to join the new command included Lt-Col Caleb V. Haynes and Maj Curtis E. LeMay, 12 other officers and 21 handpicked enlisted men. In July Lt-Col Haynes crossed the North Atlantic and in August Haynes and LeMay pioneered the South Atlantic route. In September 1941, two B-24As bedecked with highly conspicuous neutrality flags of the United States took part in the Harriman mission to Moscow via Prestwick. One continued its journey via the Middle East, India, Australia and Hawaii, and the other returned to the USA via Egypt, central Africa, the South Atlantic and Brazil. B-24A 40-2371 was one of the two, which had been fitted with cameras and three guns for a secret mission to photograph Japanese mandated islands at Jaluit, Truk and possibly Ponape, in the Pacific. It was lost at Hickam Field, Oahu, Hawaii on 7 December 1941, before Lt Ted S. Faulkner's crew could depart.

AAF B-24s enter combat

The 7th Bomb Group (BG) flew 12 Army Air Force (AAF) LB-30s to Java, and the first three AAF Liberator combat sorties were flown from there on 17 January 1942. Seventeen others, fitted with Air-to Surface Vessel (ASV) Mk II radar, hurried to the Canal Zone to supplement aircraft in the 6th BG, while six were dispatched to Hawaii and three to Alaska; these flew a

B-24D-13-CO 41-23928 on a test flight from San Diego, California in 1943. The similar B-24D 41-11822 was modified by Consolidated as the XB-41 'destroyer escort' prototype, with twin .50s in a chin turret, an additional dorsal turret behind the wing and twin .50s in each waist position, but the project was shelved after testing at Eglin in January 1943. (*via B-24 Liberator Club*)

handful of sorties in June 1942. Others served the AAF as transports, but 23 AAC LB-30s were returned to British control in 1942, bringing the RAF LB-30 total to 87. American power turrets and turbo-supercharged 1,200 hp R-1830-41 Wasps were installed on nine B-24Cs, the first of which was delivered to the AAC on 20 December 1941. The remaining Liberators on early orders became B-24Ds.

War production versions

Ordered in 1940, the B-24D was the first war-capable version to be built, being basically similar to the B-24C, but with uprated R-1830-43 engines capable of 1,200 hp at 23,400 ft. The gross weight had now reached upwards of 64,000 lb. The B-24C, and the first 82 B-24Ds produced at Consolidated's San Diego plant in 1942, were armed with seven 0.50-calibre guns: one in the nose, two in a Martin A-3 turret forward of the wing, two in the waist, and two in a Consolidated tail turret. Some 2,900 rounds of ammunition fed the guns. Three machine-guns were installed in the nose of the B-24D, and a Bendix power turret with periscopic sights provided belly protection on 179 B-24Ds. The Bendix turret was replaced later by a single hand-held tunnel gun. The bomb bay could hold up to eight 1,100-lb bombs, but the B-24D-25-CO, the B-24-10-CF, and later models, could carry eight 1,600-lb bombs. Provision was made for two 4,000-lb bombs to be mounted on underwing racks, but these were rarely carried.

The first B-24D was delivered on 23 January 1942. Contracts awarded in 1940 and subsequent orders brought the number of B-24Ds built by 1941 to 2,738. The majority of these, some 2,425 B-24Ds, were built by Consolidated-Vultee at San Diego.

In February 1941 a manufacturing pool to build B-24 Liberators was officially established. During 1942 a second Liberator production line was opened at a new Consolidated-Vultee plant at Fort Worth, Texas. This plant produced 303 B-24Ds. In March 1943 the Consolidated and Vultee companies merged, later becoming known as Convair. A third production line was started at Tulsa, Oklahoma, where Douglas Aircraft produced ten B-24Ds before changing production to 167 B-24Es.

The B-24E looked similar to the B-24D but it had different propellers and other features. The B-24G-NT, the first 25 of which were built at

A third production line was brought into operation at the Douglas Tulsa plant in Oklahoma in March 1943, beginning with 10 B-24Ds, 167 B-24Es and 25 B-24G-NTs, both of which were similar to the 'D'. (*Douglas*)

Douglas Tulsa from March 1943, was also similar in appearance to the B-24D series. Most B-24Es were used for replacement training in the US, very few being sent overseas.

Expanded construction facilities

In 1941 construction of a fourth Liberator production line by the US Government for the Ford Motor Company began at Willow Run, Dearborn, Michigan. This massive factory was 3,700,000 sq ft in area and was a quarter of a mile long, with seventy assembly lines. Completed at the end of 1942, the Ford factory at first produced B-24E aircraft and sub-assemblies for the Fort Worth and Tulsa plants. The first B-24, which was rolled out on 1 September 1942, was a Consolidated model reassembled at Willow Run. Only 490 Ford-built B-24Es were manufactured, but by the

Nose assemblies at the Douglas Tulsa plant. Ford assisted Liberator production throughout the industry, producing B-24E aircraft and sub-assemblies for both the Tulsa and Fort Worth plants. (*Douglas*)

end of 1943 later models were rolling off the lines at a rate of, on average, 340 Liberators a month. By war's end, Willow Run had produced 6,792 B-24s. This total was second only to Consolidated at San Diego, which produced 7,500 Liberators during the war.

Early in 1943, North American at Dallas, Texas began operation of the fifth and final major Liberator plant. Its first 430 Liberators were designated B-24G, and the first 25 B-24G-NTs, built at the beginning of March 1943, were very similar to the B-24D. However, experience gained in combat had revealed deficiencies in the glass-nosed B-24Ds. Like the Boeing B-17, the B-24 suffered terribly from head-on fighter attacks. *Luftwaffe* pilots, recognising that this was the bombers' most vulnerable area, took advantage of this fact and switched from rear-mounted attacks to fast-closing frontal assaults. In August 1942 a Consolidated XB-41 'escort fighter', converted from a B-24D, had been approved, but it did not enter production. It had 11,135 rounds for fourteen 0.50-calibre guns paired in a Bendix chin turret, two top turrets, tail turret, ball turret, and at each waist opening.

Better nose defences

Nose turrets had already been constructed by ingenious 5th AF engineers in Australia and by the 7th AF. They used salvaged hydraulically operated Consolidated tail turrets, installing them in the noses of B-24Ds to improve frontal firepower. In spring and summer 1943 a regular modification programme at the Hawaiian Air Depot saw over 200 Liberators for the south-west Pacific air forces receive nose turrets.

Ultimately this led to the installation of electrically powered Emerson or Consolidated nose turrets, containing two 0.50-in machine-guns, in all production B-24s. On 30 June 1943 aircraft so fitted were redesignated B-24H at Convair Fort Worth, Douglas and Ford. The change at North American, where all but the first 25 of the 430 built were fitted with Emerson nose turrets, simply brought about a block number change, and these 24s continued to be designated B-24G. These served only with the 15th AF in Italy.

A further modification saw the B-24H fitted with a Martin A-3 dorsal turret. When the K-13

and other computing gunsights were introduced, the Martin turret underwent a redesign. The A-3A 'high hat' dorsal turret had a replacement central plexiglass sighting window, with a constant-radius curvature to greatly improve sighting. A retractable Sperry ball turret, which had been introduced on late 'D' models, was also installed. Altogether, the B-24G/H carried ten 0.50-calibre guns with 4,700 rounds of ammunition, paired in the nose, top, belly and tail turrets, and at hand-operated mounts in the waist. Waist windows were provided on later blocks. Ford surprised the rest of the American aircraft industry by building no less than 1,780 B-24Hs, while Fort Worth produced 738 B-24Hs and Douglas Tulsa turned out 582 B-24H models.

Late-war Liberators

Ford also built 1,587 B-24Js. Outwardly, these were similar to the B-24H. Both 'H' and 'J' models carried Emerson turrets. A C-1 autopilot and Sperry bombsight was used on later B-24H models and the Norden M-series bombsight with C-1 autopilot was used on the B-24J. Changes were also made to the manually controlled turbo-superchargers, which were replaced with electrically controlled power boosters activated by the pilots using a single dial. These permitted much easier and smoother operation than the old pedestal-mounted controls.

Another operational problem affecting the fuel transfer system was rectified on late B-24J models. Since the early B-24D had been put into production, three auxiliary fuel cells had been added in each wing aft of the outer engines to provide an extra 450 US gallons of fuel in addition to the 2,343 US gallons normally carried, but the engines could not be fed directly from these tanks. To access the fuel the flight engineer had to transfer the fuel to main tanks first. The original fuel-transfer system was less than ideal, so a revised auxiliary fuel-tank transfer system was adopted, which reduced the risk of fire.

Convair built 738 B-24Js with the Briggs/Sperry A-13/A-13A ball turret, which had been introduced on late-production B-24Ds. A great many of these models were fitted with hydraulically operated

A B-24H-CF on flight test after being completed at Convair, Fort Worth. (*General Dynamics*)

Consolidated nose turrets, although from spring 1944, both San Diego and Fort Worth changed to Emerson nose turrets only, while Douglas built all 582 with the electrically operated Emerson turrets. The Consolidated turret, which had staggered guns, and the hydraulically operated Motor Products turret (an improved version of the Consolidated turret) could be fitted in both the nose and the tail.

Weight problems

Late in 1944 Consolidated and North American stopped using the leading edge electric/rubber de-icer boot system on the wing and tail assembly, changing to a thermal ice-preventative system, which used hot air from the engines piped to ducting inside the leading edges. These changes, and the addition of a nose turret, increased the gross weight of the aircraft to as much as 70,000 lb. Fuel consumption and overall performance suffered. With little reserve power available, take-off in particular became quite critical. It led to the ball turret being removed from some but not all Liberators in the south-west Pacific and England.

In total, Consolidated built 2,792 B-24Js. Convair built 1,558, and Douglas Tulsa built 205 B-24J-DTs. When added to the Ford figures, the

Dazzlin' Dutchess and the Ten Dukes (42-64500) was a B-24H-10-CF built by Convair. (*USAF*)

42-7652 was a B-24H-1-FO built by Ford with an Emerson nose turret. In all, Ford built 1,780 B-24Hs. Convair Fort Worth produced 738 examples and Douglas Tulsa completed 582 'H' models. (*via Mike Bailey*)

A B-24M in flight. Consolidated San Diego built 916 B-24Ms, with Ford completing 1,677. (*via Mike Bailey*)

The huge Ford plant at Willow Run at Dearborn, Michigan in full swing with B-24M-20-FOs coming off the lines. Late-version 'M's had redesigned cockpit glazing affording increased visibility, and escape panels in the roof. During the war Ford produced 6,792 B-24s and 1,893 Liberators in component form at Willow Run. (*Ford*)

five plants turned out a total of 6,678 B-24Js, the greatest number of a single Liberator variant produced.

The next variant, the B-24L, differed from previous models primarily in the installation of a much lighter tail station designed by the Convair Tucson modification centre. It weighed 200 lb less than previous turrets, and the pair of hand-held .50-in machine-guns fitted had a greater field of fire and was easier to operate. Consolidated built 417 B-24Ls at San Diego, but only 186 of these received the hand-held guns in hydraulically assisted M-6A 'Stinger' tail mounts (which were also used on some B-24Js). The rest were fitted

with standard turrets and it was not uncommon for the M-6A installation to be replaced in the field by an A-6 turret or an open twin-gun mount. Tests carried out using a Bell power boost twin .50-calibre mount in a modified B-24D nose proved quite successful but was not proceeded with because of supply problems and the impending introduction of the B-24N.

Beginning in August 1944 Ford produced 1,250 B-24Ls at Willow Run. Britain received 355 of these versions as the Liberator VIII, and they were used as heavy bombers in the Middle and Far East. RAF Coastal Command operated the B-24L in anti-submarine service. Australia

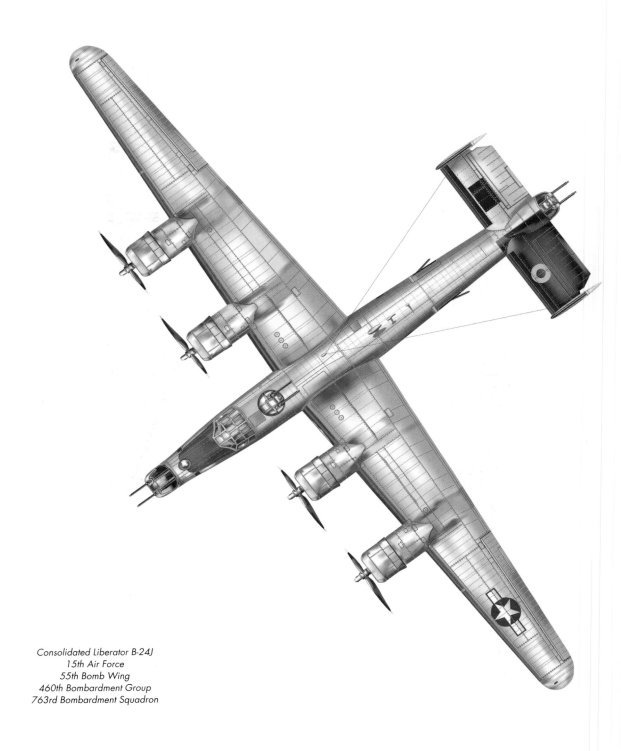

Consolidated Liberator B-24J
15th Air Force
55th Bomb Wing
460th Bombardment Group
763rd Bombardment Squadron

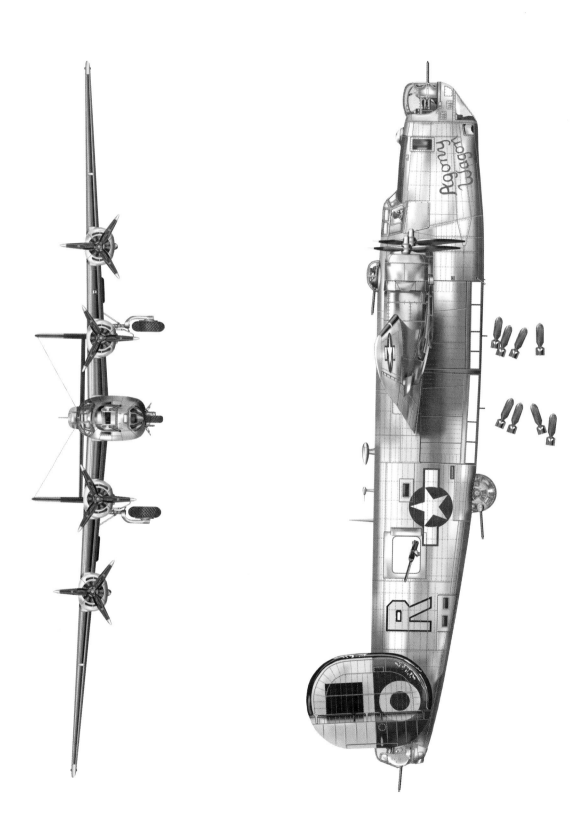

XB-24N-FO (B-24J-20-FO) 44-48753 with single tail, modified tail turret and a ball turret in the nose, which was delivered in November 1944. Ford built seven YB-24Ns and 34 were built by Consolidated to B-24N standard and delivered to the Navy under the designation RY-3. Twenty-six RY-3s were allocated to the RAF under the designation Liberator C.Mk IX. (*USN*)

received 83 B-24Ls, and Canada 16.

Convair and Ford only built the B-24N, which began to appear in early 1945. Its major distinguishing feature was the installation of lightweight turrets. Late-version 'M's had redesigned cockpit glazing affording increased visibility, and escape panels in the roof. Some 916 'M's were manufactured by Consolidated at San Diego, while 1,677 were built by Ford. Australia received more than 80, while Canada got just four. In 1945, China received 37 B-24Ms.

Single fin

Meanwhile in 1943, Ford at Willow Run modified a B-24D into the XB-24K by replacing the twin-tail empennage with a single fin and rudder. R-1830-75 engines were used, the armament fit was revised, and a ball turret was fitted to the nose. The XB-24K first flew on 9 September 1943 and underwent testing at the Eglin Field proving ground in Florida.

The single-finned machine's general stability and control was much better than in twin-finned B-24s, although it was still inferior to the B-17. It also gave an improved field of fire for the rear guns, and Eglin recommended that all

future Liberators be built with single tails. Ford built an XB-24N-FO with the single tail, which was delivered in November 1944. It was followed by seven YB-24Ns in May and June 1945, while another 34 B-24Ns were built by Consolidated and delivered to the Navy under the designation RY-3. Of the 19 retained by the Navy at the end of the war, four were used as VIP transports.

On 31 May 1945, 5,168 B-24Ns on order at Willow Run were cancelled. In July 1945 Ford modified a B-24D to create the XB-24P to test Sperry fire-control systems, and in 1946 a B-24L was modified to create the XB-24Q, to test the General Electric radar-controlled tail gun.

The peak inventory of B-24s was in September 1944, when some 6,043 Liberators were on operational strength worldwide, equipping 45 groups. At its height, the 8th AF operated 19 B-24 groups. In the Mediterranean the 15th AF operated 12 B-24 groups, and 11 more participated in the war against Japan. In spite of the aircraft's complexity, 18,482 Liberators were completed between 1941 and 1945, more than any other major American combat aircraft in history.

2. Operational History: The Pacific

The Liberator was on the verge of entering operational service in the Pacific when the Japanese launched their pre-emptive attack on the naval base at Pearl Harbor in Hawaii on 7 December 1941. Destroyed on the ground at Hickam Field was a specially modified B-24A ready to mount an armed reconnaissance of Japanese installations in the Marshalls and Carolines and particularly Truk and Jaluit. Two B-24As had been so prepared but only one had arrived when the Japanese attacked. Immediately following the attack the AAF repossessed 15 Liberators, which retained their RAF serial numbers and the LB-30 designation, and they were dispatched to the Pacific but none reached the Philippines before the Japanese occupied the islands. Four of the LB-30s reached the 7th BG in Java eventually. On 17 January 1942 three LB-30s and two B-17s from this group carried out the first AAF Liberator action of the war from airfields at Singosari, Malang, with a raid on Japanese shipping. On 12 February the 10th AF was activated for action in the CBI (China-Burma-India) theatre. On 2 April one of the repossessed LB-30s joined four B-17s for the first mission by this command in an attack on the Andaman Islands.

Deployment to India
In March 1942 the 10th AF had arrived in India with one B-24 group, the 7th. Its assorted collection of B-17s and B-24s was streamlined into a force of 35 Liberators late in 1942 and by the end of the year the 7th officially had a

strength of 32 B-24s. In reality, one squadron was still in the Middle East and two others were cadres waiting for aircraft. On 21 October 1942 the 7th BG flew its first combat mission north of the Yellow River when a flight of the 436th Bomb Squadron (BS) bombed the Lin-hsi mines. The raid, however, met with little success. By January 1943 the 7th BG was at full strength and remained on the Indian side of the Himalayas, or the 'Hump', as it was known, while the 308th BG, which was also equipped with Liberators, was sent to the Chinese side of the mountain range. The 308th was originally destined for the 8th AF but in March 1943 joined Gen Claire L. Chennault's China Task Force, which later became the 14th AF.

Over the Hump
The 308th BG was unique among B-24 groups for they had to double as transports, carrying their own supplies over the 'Hump' before flying their first mission in May 1943. Between 29 July and 20 August, the 308th flew more supply runs over the 'Hump' and then on 21 August attempted a bombing mission against Hankow. However, the 14 B-24s missed their rendezvous with a group of P-40 escort fighters and in a battle with up to 100 Japanese fighters, three Liberators were shot down. The disaster was repeated on the 24th when four were lost.

In November 1943 South East Asia Command (SEAC) was activated under the command of Admiral the Lord Louis Mountbatten. Maj-Gen George E. Stratemeyer was appointed chief of Eastern Air Command,

B-24Ds of the 28th Composite Group, 11th AF, landing in the Aleutians after a raid against Japanese targets in the North Pacific. (*USAF*)

which effectively united the British and American air forces. Stratemeyer proposed using the combined strength of the 7th and 308th BGs in a mission against vital installations around Rangoon. The 308th was moved temporarily to India and the strike was scheduled for 25 November, but the raid, involving the B-24s, B-25 Mitchells and fighters, went badly wrong. The fighters were prevented from taking off because of bad weather (which also caused the loss of two B-24s on take-off) and the heavies proceeded alone. The targets were covered in overcast and bombing results were poor. A third B-24 was lost over the target.

Further raids were made, and results were more successful. Right up until the end of the war British and American B-24s worked in co-operation. In January 1944, the combined forces could call on almost 80 Liberators. It had been planned to transfer the 10th and 14th AF to the Pacific to co-ordinate with the Far East Air Forces (FEAF) in the Philippines but the war ended before the transfer could be made.

Next to see action in the Pacific was the 11th AF in Alaska. The 36th BS had one LB-30 at the end of 1941 but received more B-24s by June 1942, when the 21st BS arrived. The small 11th AF had the onerous task of defending Alaska and the Aleutian Island chain in the Bering Sea. The 11th had its advanced base on Umnak

Island, 2,400 miles from Anchorage in Alaska.

The Japanese held the other end of the Aleutians, at Attu and Kiska. The enemy believed that this would be an effective deterrent for any US invasion of Japan through the Aleutians and the Kuriles, but they need not have worried. The Aleutian chain, with its horrendous weather and unforgiving terrain, was a totally unsuitable place from which to mount any invasion of Japan. On 10 June four B-24s and the single LB-30 took off from Cold Bay, Alaska and flew to Umnak to load up their bombs for an attack on enemy shipping in Kiska Harbor. The attack met with little success. One B-24 was shot down by flak and two others were badly damaged. Between June and October 1942, the 11th AF lost 72 aircraft. It is an indication of the kind of weather experienced in this theatre that of these, only nine were combat losses.

Arctic patrols

Late in 1942, B-24Ds of the 404th BS joined the 36th and the 21st in the Aleutians. This squadron was known as the 'Pink Elephants' because its Liberators were painted desert-pink, having been originally intended for the North African theatre! The 404th was very successful, flying 39 patrols over the Bering Sea without loss. Throughout 1943 the 11th AF raided

Japanese shipping and bases in the Aleutians from a new base at Adak, only 250 miles from Kiska. Amchitka was successfully invaded on 5 January, and on 1 July the B-24s flew a 1,700-mile round-trip from Adak to Paramishiro in the Kuriles. A second mission to Paramishiro was flown on 11 August 1943. Four days later Kiska was invaded, and on 11 September a mixed force of seven B-24Ds and 12 B-25 Mitchells again bombed Paramishiro. Ten aircraft failed to return and the badly depleted 11th AF could only train for raids on the Kuriles later in the New Year, when they would be joined by some F-7 Liberators of the 2nd Photo Charting Squadron.

The Pacific War

The air war over the enormous expanse of the Pacific Ocean, from Hawaii to the Philippines, and Australia to the Japanese mainland, was divided between three air forces: the 5th, 7th and 13th. Maj-Gen Clarence L. Tinker, who in June 1942 was CO of the small 7th AF, headquartered on Midway Island, realised the great possibilities in using the long-ranging Liberator and was determined to have it in his inventory. In a demonstration of the B-24's capabilities, Tinker put forward the idea of bombing Wake Island, 1,250 miles distant, using four LB-30s which had landed at Midway after leaving Hawaii on 5 June. They refuelled at Midway and in the evening of the 6th took off again for Wake Island loaded with every drop of fuel the LB-30s could hold and carrying six 500-lb bombs apiece. Thirty minutes after take-off Tinker's LB-30, with Lt Hinton at the controls, nosed forward into some overcast and was never seen again. The three others bombed Wake Island successfully. It was the first of many similar strikes. Tinker's crews did not share his regard for the B-24 and they were deeply concerned when the 7th began equipping with the Liberator instead of the B-17. Tinker's successor, Gen Willis H. Hale, had a difficult task in persuading his crews that accepting the B-24 did not make the 7th AF a second-class outfit. Gradually, the crews grew to accept the long-ranging bomber and Tinker's early enthusiasm as justified.

On 22 December 1942 Col William A. Matheny, CO, 307th BG, led 26 B-24Ds on another mission from Midway to Wake. The B-24s bombed at varied heights from 7,000 ft to 25,000 ft, and the only damage to the American formation was two small holes in the lead ship. Later, the 307th BG, better known as the 'Long Rangers', were transferred to the 13th AF and some of their B-24Ds were taken on charge by the 11th BG, which replaced them at Hawaii. The 11th BG flew their first mission to Wake via Midway on 26 July 1943.

A line of longitude placed the 5th AF on the south-west Pacific side and the 13th AF, activated in December 1942, on the South

The B-24 *Virgin II* of the 90th 'Jolly Rogers' BG of the 5th AF in New Guinea, on 9 December 1942. The 90th BG had arrived from Hawaii in September 1941 and had been assigned to the 7th AF while it completed training. In October 1942 it transferred to the 5th AF in Australia, thus becoming the first complete group to reach the south-west Pacific. The Group flew its first mission on 16 November 1942 to Bougainville Island. (*USAF*)

A B-24D of the 308th BG, 14th AF, takes off from Kunming, China in 1943. The 308th BG, the only B-24 group based in China, supported operations by Chinese ground forces, bombed land targets in Burma and Indo-China, and sank shipping in the China Seas, the Gulf of Tonkin and the Taiwan Strait. (*USAF*)

Pacific side. The 5th AF fought in the Philippines at the outbreak of the Pacific war and covered the retreat south to Java, playing a small part in the Battle of the Coral Sea.

It really came to prominence late in 1942, when Gen George C. Kenney assumed command. Kenney had four B-24 groups by the end of the war: the 90th 'Jolly Rogers', 43rd 'Ken's Men'; 380th 'Flying Circus' and the 22nd 'Red Raiders'. The 90th BG had moved hurriedly to Hawaii in September 1941 and was assigned to the 7th AF while it completed training. In October 1942 it transferred to the 5th AF in Australia, thus becoming the first complete group to reach the south-west Pacific. The Group flew its first mission on 16 November 1942 – a raid on Bougainville Island. By the beginning of 1943 the 'Jolly Rogers', as they were known after their CO, Col Arthur Rogers, were flying long-range missions to targets in Celebes and Java. The 380th, part of the 5th AF, was attached to the RAAF until January 1945 and among its regular tasks was training Australian B-24 crews for the RAAF.

Night raiders

The two B-24 groups in the 13th AF were the 307th 'Long Rangers' and the 5th 'Bomber Barons'. Late in August 1943 a special unit of ten SB-24 Liberators, known as the 'Snoopers', joined the 5th BG as the 349th BS and, equipped with new radar bombsights, they flew missions

B-24D-50-CO 42-40323 *Frenisi* of the 307th BG, 13th AF is seen on Los Negros, having flown 110 missions. It was about to depart for the US, where the crew were to help the War Bond drive. (*USAF*)

against Japanese shipping almost every night from 27 August onwards. The strikes became known as the 'Tokyo Express' and such was their success that a new squadron, the 868th, was activated in January 1944 and this unit operated independently in the 13th AF.

On 11 October 1943, Hawaii greeted the arrival of the 30th BG. Despite having had only a few weeks' training the 30th was declared ready to participate in Operation *Galvanic*, the invasion of the Japanese-held Gilbert Islands (now Kiribati), 2,000 miles from Hawaii. Three squadrons of the 11th BG also took part, flying out of the Ellis Islands. Between 14 November and 6 December 1943, the 7th AF flew 29 missions to establish air superiority over Tarawa, losing seven Liberators.

In January 1944 the B-24s of the 7th AF took part in Operation *Flintlock*, the 70-day pre-invasion bombardment of the largest atoll in the world, Kwajalein. Altogether, *Flintlock* cost 7th Bomber Command 18 Liberators. The 7th, now established at Tarawa, rapidly earned a reputation for carrying out tough, specialist

tasks and the next assigned to it was bomber support during Operation *Catchpole*, the invasion of Eniwetok and the Marshalls. The first heavy strikes were made on 17 February and successive raids by Liberators of the 7th AF and Navy PB4Ys neutralised Japanese air bases in the Marshalls and the Carolines. The island of Truk in the Carolines became a regular mission for 7th AF crews and by late February 1944 the island had been largely neutralised.

Action in the Pacific

At the end of March 1944 all three army air forces had bombed Japanese airfields and positions on Ponape, Kusiae, Kapingamangari, and New Guinea. Navy PB4Y-1s had raided Palau, Yap and Woleai. By April, the 11th and 30th BGs were based on Kwajalein and, together with the Navy and the 5th and 13th AFs, they had largely destroyed most Japanese air bases east of the Philippines. That same month seven 30th BG B-24s flew a shuttle bombing mission of more than 4,000 miles with PB4Y-1s on a triangular route from Eniwetok to

The US Navy's first Liberators were PB4Y-1 models from the B-24D production lines at San Diego, California. B-24D-7-CO 41-23827 became BuNo. 31937, the second PB4Y-1 assigned to the Navy. (*General Dynamics*)

the Carolines and bombing Guam in the Marianas. On 15 May B-24s of 7th Bomber Command, together with other aircraft, began round-the-clock bombing of Japanese positions in the Marshalls, ending with the destruction of all targets by the end of the month.

Navy Liberators

Early in World War 2 the US Navy recognised the need for a very-long-range patrol aircraft, heavily armed and armoured, which could be used in 'masthead' attacks on Japanese shipping. On 7 July 1942 the AAF agreed to the Navy receiving a quantity of PB4Y-1 versions of the B-24D and these began reaching operational units in August. In August 1943 the AAF's Anti-Submarine Command was disbanded and all ASV-equipped B-24Ds were handed over to the USN as PB4Y-1s in exchange for an equal number of unmodified B-24s already in production. In all, the USN received 1,174 Liberators, equipping 32 squadrons. At its peak the USN operated 20 bomber squadrons in the Atlantic and Pacific theatres.

Though a complex and demanding aircraft, the PB4Y-1 was without doubt the finest patrol bomber of the war. Outwardly it looked identical to the B-24. The first PB4Y-1 squadron

was VB-101, 'V' being the Navy code applied to units flying heavier-than-air machines. Together with VB-102 and a Marine photo squadron, VB-101 was ordered to the forward area in the South Pacific. On 10 April 1943 VB-104 was commissioned. In August, at Carney Field, Guadalcanal it formed the first Navy Long-Range Search Group along with VB-102. The primary role was daily search and tracing of enemy task force units but a large number of formation strikes were made against land targets, and one strike against a Japanese destroyer fleet. Individual strikes were made when the opportunity arose.

By now known as VPB-104 (PB standing for Patrol Bomber), the squadron moved to Munda Field, New Georgia on 6 February 1944. At the end of March the 'Buccaneers of Screaming 104' were relieved by VPB-115 after having flown over 1,000 sorties and destroying or damaging 30 aircraft and 51 enemy surface vessels for the loss of only seven Liberators. On 15 May 1944 VPB-104 was re-formed and at Morotai in the Netherlands East Indies on 3 November they relieved VPB-115. VPB-104 and VPB-l0l, also equipped with PB4Y-1s and VPB-146, equipped with PV-ls, now formed the Navy Search Group attached to the Seventh Fleet.

A USN PB4Y-1 (B-24J) Liberator. Note the Engineering Research Company (ERCO) nose turret, known as a bow turret in naval circles. (*General Dynamics*)

Navy Liberator crews were devastating in their low-level strafing and bombing runs on enemy shipping at masthead height. Here, a Japanese ship burns after an attack by a PB4Y-1 of VB-104, flown by Lt Paul F. Stevens. The squadron became famous as the 'Buccaneers of Screaming 104'. (*Stevens*)

B-24s of the 11th BG, 7th AF taxi out onto the crushed coral runway of their island base in May 1944. (USAF)

Lt Paul F. Stevens, an experienced patrol plane commander, recalls:

'VPB-104 had arrived at Morotai with 18 flight crews and 15 PB4Y-1s. The B-24J was an excellent choice for our mission. Painted Navy blue, there were several modifications and additions to the basic Liberator. The two forward bomb bays were loaded permanently with 390-gallon fuel tanks. These tanks were self-sealing which reduced the usable number of gallons available to about 300 each. These tanks could be jettisoned in an emergency. The total usable fuel load for our maximum range search missions was 3,400 gallons according to our Aircraft Action Reports. The maximum design weight for a bomber mission was 56,000 lb, but we flew our airplanes on search missions as high as 68,000 lbs at takeoff. Our bomb load varied but was usually limited to 1,500 lb carried in the two aft bomb bays. We carried a mix of 100-, 250- and 500-lb high explosive bombs with four-to five-second delayed fuses. Most of the bombs were general-purpose (GP) high explosives (HE). However, the 100-lb incendiary clusters were found to be very effective against the small wooden ships of the Sugar Dog and Sugar Puppy classes. The

incendiary clusters did not work very well at all when dropped on the larger steel-hulled vessels. Occasionally, and particularly on the shorter patrols, extra 100-lb high explosive and/or incendiary cluster bombs were carried loosely stowed on the bomb bay walkways and alongside the nose wheel crawl space. Loading these extra bombs while in flight required very strong-armed crewmen.

PB4Y guns

'Initially, all but three of our PB4Y-1s were equipped with four powered twin 0.50 caliber machine gun turrets and two single 0.50 caliber machine guns in the waist hatches. These airplanes and most replacement airplanes had the belly turret removed and an APS-15 radar installed. The bow turret was manufactured by the Engineering Research Company (ERCO) and was an exceptionally fine gun turret. The top turret was supplied by Sperry and Martin, the Martin being the better of the two. Sperry supplied the belly turrets. The tail turret was built by Consolidated Aircraft Company, which also manufactured most of our Liberators.

'On all patrols we carried extra 0.50 caliber ammunition and gun barrels. Due to the experience of the first combat tour, extra feed motors were installed for the tail turret. The feed trays for the tail turret were 14 ft long. After the patrol the guns were broken down, cleaned and the head spacing checked.'

'To a man, we were strongly against the removal of the belly turret. We wanted all the firepower we could get. Even so, the APS-15 radar did prove to be most valuable for the search mission. The scope presented a 360° pattern and gave a good positioning of a target. It was also a great assist with our navigation. Land mass targets could be identified at ranges of 100 nautical miles or so and 'mapped'. Large ships gave a return at 25 to 50 nm, dependent upon aircraft altitude, atmospheric conditions, and no heavy weather around the target area. Heavy weather would blank out a ship's return on the scope.

'The airplanes with the belly turrets had the ASE radar. Two array antennas were mounted low on the forward hull just aft of the bow turret, one on each side. The antennas could be rotated from dead ahead through 90° to both beams. Detection ranges were about the same though the ASE did not paint the weather nor did it 'map' a land mass. Once a target was detected, it was necessary to head the airplane in the direction of the target and balance the returns on the scope to home in on the target.

'The last three airplanes delivered were also equipped with an ECM device, as were some of the replacement airplanes. These passive devices received both radar transmissions and VHF radio signals. By heading the airplane in the direction of the transmitted signal, one could home in on the station. This proved to be of considerable value. It did require a radar technician for operations.

Reliable powerplants

'The Pratt & Whitney R-1830-65 engines served us very well. Turbo-supercharged, they could deliver full power all the way up to service ceiling. Electronically controlled, it was a simple twist of the graduated knob to demand power even above the maximum allowed for the engines. Beat the engines as we did, the reliability was excellent, especially considering the tropical operating conditions. However, at around 500 hours run time we did begin to experience engine problems. A turbo by-pass feature permitted the pilot to by-pass the turbo and rely upon the basic engine mechanical supercharger to generate the 1,200 hp for takeoff. This did help with controlling cylinder head temperatures somewhat. One final nicety was the auxiliary power unit (APU or "putt-putt") which helped with starting the engines and servicing the airplane.'

B-24J-5-CO 42-73029 of the 11th BG over Kwajalein, Marshall Islands, in June 1944. (USAF)

A B-24J of the 11th BG, 7th AF overflies Makin Island, one of the Tarawa group of atolls. (*USAF*)

Lt Earl Bittenbender, plane commander, Crew 13, PB4Y-1 BuNo. 38856 in VPB-104, recalls a low-level bombing and strafing attack on a Sugar Dog – a small cargo ship of 200 tons – off Ishigaki-Shima. The island was a haven for the Sugar Dog class of Japanese vessels.

'On this rainy day on Sector Six covering the Ryukyus…on the return flight, I decided to bomb a Sugar Dog several miles from a small island. I told the bow gunner to stop firing within a half mile of the target in case it would explode from our bullets. Not getting the message, he fired until we went over it at about thirty feet. The bomb missed so we came around for another run. Since there was no

explosion due to the strafing on the first run, I said nothing about not firing close in to the ship. On this attack, just before the bow of the airplane was over the ship, it exploded and we flew through flying lumber. A piece from the bow turret's Plexiglas passed by our windshield and we emerged from the flying debris with the starboard engines and wing shaking. Looking over and beyond the left-hand outboard engine, I could see a large gash in the leading edge of the wing, probably where the ship's masthead came up and hit the wing. I feared that the wing would break off and the aircraft would cartwheel through the water and kill us all. So I added power to climb high

B-24 4047 of the 20th Combat Mapping Squadron, 5th AF in the south-west Pacific. (*B-24 Liberator Club*)

enough to get our parachute harnesses on and then bail out. Adding power created two loud backfires and the after station said the No. 3 engine was on fire. I cut the throttle, fuel, and ignition, and feathered the engine and was able to continue the climb. It appeared that the debris had damaged the exhaust stack, jamming the super-charger control vent, thereby causing excessive intake manifold pressure. This exploded one of the cylinders into three pieces.

'With only three engines and a badly damaged airplane, I decided to try and make Lingayen Gulf airstrip as it was closer than Tacloban. We planned to jettison the forward bomb bay fuel tanks once we had land in sight. If we were forced to ditch before then, these tanks would have provided extra flotation. After landing at Lingayen there was no question that PB4Y-l BuNo. 38856 would never fly again but by God's grace, the crew did…'

Oil targets
In September 1944 Liberators of the 5th AF in the New Guinea campaign flew missions against the oil refineries at Balikpapan in Borneo. The 'Ploesti of the Pacific' was only second in production to Palembang in Sumatra.

The first raid on the Balikpapan oilfields had been made by B-24s of the 380th BG on 13 August 1943 in a 17-hour sortie from Darwin, Australia. Two further raids were made before in September 1944 the airfield at Noemfoor in north-west New Guinea became available, reducing the flying time to 14 hours and allowing the B-24s to carry a 2,500-lb bomb load. The 5th and 307th BGs were moved to New Guinea and on 30 September 46 Liberators from these two groups bombed Balikpapan. Defending Japanese fighters shot down three B-24s. On 3 October the 13th AF tried again and seven B-24s of the 307th BG were shot down. Nineteen B-24s of the 5th BG survived completely unscathed. Further raids by a combined force of 5th and 13th AF groups, and fighters, caused great damage to the plant. In a total of five raids on the plant, 22 Liberators were lost.

Maximising range
Meanwhile, on 30 September, 72 B-24s of the 5th, 90th and 307th BGs had carried out the first of a series of raids in which optimum range was achieved by such devices as moving crewmen from one part of the aircraft to another at given times and firing all remaining

B-24Js of the 7th BG attack the Bilin railroad bridge in Burma on 13 November 1944. (*USAF*)

B-24J-10-CO *Tropic Knight,* seen on Saipan in the Mariana Islands in 1944. Note the Consolidated A-6A nose turret with wind deflector fitted on the side. (*USAF*)

The crew of the Liberator *Bombs Nip On* in the Pacific theatre smile for the camera. (via *Mike Bailey*)

ammunition soon after leaving the target. Also in September, the 5th and 13th AFs, collectively known as the Far East Air Force, began attacks on the Philippines and supported the island-hopping campaign across the Pacific.

The 494th BG, known as 'Kelly's Cobras' after its CO, Col Laurence Kelly, was the last B-24 group to be activated in World War 2, and from October 1944 operated with the 7th AF over the Philippines. It took part in many strikes on such targets as Clark Field, Bataan, Corregidor and Manila. When the Philippines fell on 16 February 1945, the 'Cobras' flew raids in support of the guerrilla forces. From August 1944 until 19 February 1945 the 11th and 30th BGs, 7th AF were engaged in strikes on Iwo Jima and surrounding islands.

By July 1945 all the Pacific air forces had begun moving northward for the final assault on Japan. The 43rd BG was based on Ie Shima and attacking targets on Kyushu, southernmost of the Japanese home islands. Just over 100 B-24s in the 22nd, 90th and 380th BGs, 5th AF

were based at Okinawa. The 11th and 30th BGs moved up to the Ryuku Islands. The two 13th AF groups, the 5th and 307th, had moved to Clark Field in the Philippines, and had begun attacking targets in Taiwan and Indo-China.

Bombing Japan

All three groups in the 5th AF flew explosive and fire raids on Japan but the honour of being the first group in the AAF to bomb Japan went to the 'Cobras' of the 494th BG, when its B-24s raided Omura Airfield on Kyushu. The armed forces of Japan were now being attacked from all sides. On 19 June 1945 11th AF B-24s completed a 2,700-mile trip from Shamya Kruppa. The 11th AF flew its last mission on 13 August 1945 with a raid on Parasmishiro in the Kuriles.

The war in Europe was over. There was speculation that the bomber groups of the 8th AF would be sent to the Pacific, but the atomic bomb made such reinforcement redundant, and the 5th, 7th and 13th Air Forces disbanded.

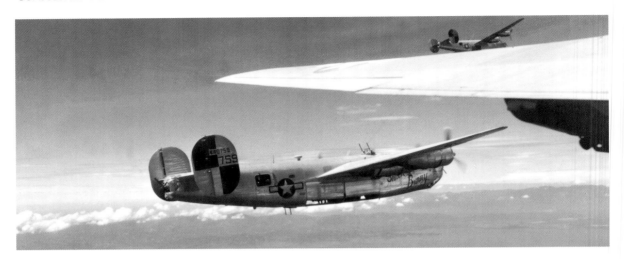

B-24J-180-CO *Shack Bunny* of the 867th BS, 494th BG, 7th AF over the Gulf of Java. It is *en route* to bomb the Japanese airfield at Mintal on Mindanao, Philippines, in March 1945. (*USAF*)

B-24M-15-CO and B-24J-170-CO of the 494th BG, 7th AF approaching their target. They are about to attack Japanese positions located in a partially wooded area six miles west of Cebu City, Cebu Island in the Philippines, on 25 March 1945. (*USAF*)

3. Operational History: ETO and the Mediterranean

By the end of August 1942 over 100 B-17s – enough for three groups – had arrived in Britain. On 17 August, the 8th Air Force flew its first heavy bomber mission of the war, when a handful of Fortresses were dispatched to north-eastern France where they bombed a large marshalling yard. B-17 crews threw themselves headlong into a bitter war over Europe in daylight and without escort. The European effort was not without opposition, particularly from the Navy, which was convinced that America's first objective lay in the defeat of Japan.

In September 1942, plans to introduce the B-24 into Europe went ahead. Seventeen B-24D Liberators of the 93rd BG flew into Alconbury in Huntingdonshire but did not fly their first mission until 9 October, when they attacked the Fives-Lille steelworks in Belgium. This was the first mission flown by the 8th AF from East Anglia in which over 100 bombers participated. Col Ted Timberlake, CO, 93rd BG, flying *Teggie Ann*, led 24 B-24Ds to the target behind the larger formation of B-17s. One aircraft was lost over France and only ten B-24s hit their target.

At the end of the month two of the squadrons in the 93rd BG went on detached duty to Coastal Command. During October B-24Ds of the 44th BG began arriving at Shipdham, Norfolk. These two Liberator groups, along with four B-17 groups, had to prove conclusively that daylight precision bombing in Europe could succeed.

Many senior Allied officers were not convinced that unescorted bombers could bomb in daylight and survive against German opposition. Soon .50-calibre machine-guns were being installed in the vulnerable nose section to combat the head-on approach of the *Luftwaffe* fighters. Automatic belt feed systems were introduced on all machine-gun armament, replacing the cumbersome process of changing 36-round drums by hand. Some armament officers even installed twin 'fifties' in the glass nose area, which were fired by bombardiers and navigators lying on their stomachs. The *Luftwaffe* soon developed a healthy respect for the new armament.

Missions over Europe

On 7 November 1942 the 44th BG, the 'Flying Eightballs', carried out its first combat mission when eight B-24Ds flew a diversionary sweep for B-17s attacking positions in Holland. Two days later, 35 B-17s followed by 12 B-24Ds, flying over the sea at 500 ft to avoid enemy radar, climbed to between 7,500 ft and 18,000 ft to bomb the U-boat pens at St Nazaire, France. The Fortresses suffered losses but the B-24s, bombing from 18,000 ft, came through intact. It was unusual for the Liberators to be above the B-17s: the B-24's high wing loading made it difficult to maintain formation above 21,000 ft. Its service ceiling was officially 28,000 ft, about 4,000 ft below the optimum Fortress altitude.

The B-24D's operational cruising speed of 180 mph was almost 20 mph faster than a B-17 and it caused many problems in mission planning. Usually it meant that the Liberators flew behind the B-17 formations.

B-24D Liberators of the 'Flying Eightballs', the 44th BG, bomb Dunkirk harbour on 15 February 1943. (*USAF*)

One solution was for B-17 and B-24 groups to be flown separately. While the 93rd BG operated from North Africa between December 1942 and February 1943, the 44th BG flew mostly diversionary sweeps for the B-17s. However, when they accompanied the Forts, as they did on 3 January 1943 to St Nazaire once more, the performance differences between the two big bombers again caused problems.

Bombing accuracy had long been a concern, and the 8th AF abandoned individual bombing in favour of group bombing on this raid. When the 68 B-17s reached the target the eight B-24Ds flying in the rear had caught up. They were higher than the Fortresses and their bombs passed through the B-17 formations. On the next mission, to the shipyards at Kiel, on 14 May, the 44th's cargo of incendiaries required a shorter trajectory and a longer bomb run than the B-17s. Flying a scattered formation the Liberators were exposed to fighter attack. Five B-24s, including three in the 67th BS, which brought up the rear of the formation, were shot down before they could release their bombs.

Ploesti attacked

On 29 May the B-24Ds were taken off operations to train for Operation *Tidal Wave*, a daring low-level raid on the Ploesti oilfields in Romania. Early in June a third group, the 389th

'Sky Scorpions' arrived in Norfolk for training for the raid, which would also involve the 98th and 376th – the two 9th AF B-24D groups in Libya. Missions were flown in support of the *Torch* operation before Ploesti was attacked from North Africa on 1 August by 177 B-24D Liberators of the 44th, 93rd, 98th, 389th and 376th BGs. Malfunctions and accidents *en route* reduced the effectiveness of the force and navigational errors caused severe problems in the target area, forcing some groups to bomb each other's assigned targets. Delayed-action bombs from preceding groups damaged or destroyed Liberators in the following groups; 167 actually attacked their targets and dropped 311 tons of bombs on the refineries. Some 54 B-24Ds were lost over the targets and three more crashed into the sea. Seven B-24D crews were interned in Turkey, while 19 landed in Cyprus, Sicily or Malta. Of the 92 that returned to North Africa, 55 had suffered battle damage.

The intensity and suicidal nature of the raid was such that five Medals of Honor were awarded for actions on the Ploesti mission, three of them posthumously. The drama shared by all is succinctly captured by 1/Lt John B. McCormick in the 565th BS, 389th BG and pilot of the *Vagabond King*, whose target was 'Red I' – Steaua Romana, the second largest refinery, at Campina, Ploesti.

B-24Ds of the 44th BG, 8th AF over Kiel, Germany on 14 May 1943. (*USAF*)

'Everything looked good. Things never look dangerous when you have so much company. We even felt secure in the rear guard...We called ourselves "The Cluster On The Purple Heart Squadron". Then, out of a blue sky, without warning, the leading plane of another group up front spun sickeningly out of formation, and exploded against the sea, burning, so as to leave a black tomb marker. The second ship down, before we had even touched enemy land. Immediately, all gunners got itchy looking for a possible fighter...Then another B-24 peeled off, heading home, one engine feathered. That was the hot desert putting in its two cents worth. We looked to our giant engines, but they gave no indication of weakening under the heavy load we carried.'

'...And down we dropped, to silhouette our target against the sky, just like Mosco and I had practiced on the model area, simulating Ploesti, they had built for us on the desert in Libya...we turned to the North again, ready to make the

'Red I' Steaua Romana, the second-largest refinery, at Campina, Ploesti, on fire on 1 August 1943 after being hit by bombs dropped by 26 B-24Ds of the 389th 'Sky Scorpions' BG led by Col Jack Wood, CO, and Maj Kenneth 'Fearless' Caldwell. 'Red' target was completely destroyed. (*via Earl Zimmerman*)

The Columbia Aquila refinery – target 'White V' – burns from bombs released by 17 B-24Ds of the 44th BG, 8th AF, led by Col Leon Johnson and Maj Bill Brandon in B-24 *Suzy Q*. 'White V' was put out of action for 11 months. Another 19 'Flying Eightball' B-24Ds, led by Col Jim Posey, completely destroyed 'Blue Target' – the Creditul Minier Brazi, 5 miles to the south of Ploesti. (*USAF*)

final approach and bomb run. I warmed up my fixed nose-guns with a loud burst that startled Mosco so much he almost jumped out of the nose. We were ready for strafing now. For the first time in history B-24s were going to be used on a strafing run. We turned South down the valley. The lead plane had already started his bomb run. Christ! His plane was already burning, and he was carrying thousand pound bombs... with delayed fuses! Then it was "Gunners, keep your eyes open for fighters and ack-ack batteries." "Don't shoot civilians unless they're throwing bottles at us! Mosco, bomb-bay doors open."

'Bang! What the Hell? Here we go anyway...down on the carpet...we get right behind, and under Stan Podalak's plane... Mooney's left wing... We line up our two chimneys, which will put our bombs right through the windows of the boiler house. We can't drop far behind Mooney's plane 'cause he's carrying 45 second delay fuses...same as we are. Above us, we could look into Stan's open bomb bay doors...we could see the bombs hanging ready, willing, and able. Tracers...red...white...were streaming up at the boys ahead...hitting them, too! Then our cockpit exploded with sparks, noise, and concussion...tracers spat out over my head. George and I crouched down, making ourselves as small as possible. The tracers melted away into the smoke and fire of the refinery. Murphy cut loose in the top gun turret, with the twin 50s...I wanted to shoot him...he was ruining our bomb run!

Bombing at ground level

'Wham! More bullets through the cockpit! The emergency windows blew open, giving us a 225-mph blast of air in the cockpit. But now, we were down to almost ground level, lined up and anxious to go. We came up to the target chimney height and through the smoke...over the other bomb explosions...then...BOMBS AWAY! Our plane was now 4,000 lb lighter...Three minutes after "bombs away" the boys told me we had been hit pretty hard...Van was bleeding badly. An AA cannon shell had hit his knee as he was turning on the automatic camera...Miller, in the tin-can – the tail-turret – called to say that the bombs we dropped, had exploded, and our target was flattened and burning fiercely...'

'Red I' was destroyed by bombs dropped by 26 B-24Ds of the 389th BG led by Col Jack Wood and Maj Kenneth 'Fearless' Caldwell. Though 42 per cent of the Ploesti's refining capacity and 40 per cent of its cracking capacity were claimed destroyed, most of the refineries were soon repaired and were operating at pre-mission capacity again within a month. All five groups received Presidential Unit Citations. The AAF was to lose more than 200 bombers and over 2,000 aircrew in raids on the Ploesti refineries before the end of the war in Europe.

At the end of August, after more raids from Benghazi, the three 8th AF groups were ordered back to Norfolk, where they joined the newly arrived 392nd BG equipped with B-24Hs and Js

A B-24D of the 98th BG, 9th AF flies low over the Astra Romana refinery, the most modern and the largest at Ploesti. The 'Pyramiders' suffered the highest casualties on 1 August 1943, losing 21 of the 38 Liberators that began the low-level mission. (*USAF*)

with power-operated nose turrets. The Wendling group was soon joined by the similarly equipped 445th, 446th, 448th, and 453rd BGs, though the Division was still not strong enough to mount deep-penetration raids without fighter escort. The 445th flew its first mission on 13 December 1943 in a raid on Kiel. Three days later the 446th flew its first mission in the raid on Bremen, while the 448th BG flew its first mission on 22 December.

New blood at the top

Gen Jimmy Doolittle took command of the 8th AF on 1 January 1944. His directive was simple: 'Win the air war and isolate the battlefield!' In other words: 'Destroy the *Luftwaffe* and cut the Normandy beaches for the Invasion.' On 24 February a force of 235 Liberators attacked the Bf 110 assembly plant at Gotha. Despite relays of escorts – three Thunderbolt groups escorted

the B-24s to near Hanover and then the P-38 Lightnings and P-51 Mustangs orbited the formation as it proceeded to Gotha – losses were heavy. Over 150 enemy fighters attacked the formation all the way to the target and Fw 190s, Bf 110s, Bf 210s, and Ju 88s raked the American formations with cannon- and rocket-fire. Homing in on the Liberator's thick vapour trails to excellent advantage, they often struck at lagging bombers from below and behind. The *Luftwaffe* even attempted to disrupt the large and unwieldy combat wings.

By this time the 445th BG had lost eight B-24s, five of which were shot down in just six minutes. When the Division changed course to the south-east with a feint towards Meinegen, confusion arose at the initial point. The navigator in the 389th BG lead ship suffered oxygen failure and veered off course and the bombardier slumped over his sight and accidentally tripped the bombs. Twenty-five Liberators bombed the secondary target at Eisenach. By the time the 445th formation reached the target its losses were now 12 B-24s fallen to the German guns, and only 13 Liberators remained. Realising that they had veered off course, the surviving aircraft of the 445th continued to Gotha alone where they executed an eight-minute bomb run, dropping 180 500-pounders from 12,200 ft. Another 171 B-24s dropped 468 tons on the Bf 110 plant, causing widespread damage. It was estimated that six to seven weeks' production would be lost. However, The 445th had lost 13 B-24s and 122 men on the mission. Seven 392nd BG B-24s were missing and 13 were damaged.

By March 1944 the 2nd BD had increased to eleven groups with the 458th, 466th, and 467th BGs forming the 96th Combat Wing. During April five more B-24 groups landed in England and despite the obvious drawbacks of mixing two types of heavy bomber, they joined the 3rd BD, hitherto equipped with the Fortress.

Doolittle wanted to bring the Eighth up to strength with Fortresses but there were simply not enough to go round. In contrast, by the late spring of 1944, five B-24 plants in America were producing more than enough Liberators, and hundreds of them were needed for D-Day, the invasion of Western Europe.

Stand-off glide bomb

In the build-up to the invasion the Azon VB-1 (VB standing for Vertical Bomb) 'stand-off' glide weapon made its appearance. It was carried by the 753rd BS in the 458th BG. The bomb was a 1,000- or 2,000-lb GP bomb fitted with radio-controlled movable tail fins. After release, a flare in the tail ignited and kept it in view of the controller in a 'mother ship', who steered the bomb, in the horizontal plane only, by radio. Used mainly against bridges in France the Azon project began on 30 May when four B-24s failed to hit a bridge spanning the Loire. The project was soon abandoned,

B-24Hs and Js of the 446th BG, 8th AF heading for the Messerschmitt Bf 110 plant at Gotha, Germany on 24 February 1944, during 'Big Week'. Some 238 B-24s from eight groups bombed the plant. The 392nd BG dropped 98 per cent of its bombs within 2,000 ft of the mean point of impact, and the 44th BG also achieved a highly accurate bomb run. It was estimated that the raid cost the Germans six to seven weeks' Bf 110 production. (*USAF*)

B-24J-1-DT 42-51258 of the 492nd BG, piloted by 2/Lt Karl W. Ruthenbeck, is seen over the Schulau oil refinery near Hamburg on 6 August 1944. This was the ill-fated group's penultimate mission of the war. The next day the group was withdrawn from combat having lost 54 B-24s in just three months from May 1944, the heaviest loss suffered by any Liberator group over such a short period. (*USAF*)

although late in 1944 the Azon was employed in Burma against bridges. The 7th BG in the CBI theatre claimed 27 bridges with 459 Azon bombs and direct hits with 10–15 per cent of those dropped.

A total of 2,362 8th AF B-24 and B-17 sorties were flown on D-Day, 6 June. The first missions were primarily concerned with the neutralising of enemy coastal defences and front-line troops. The second and third missions were directed against lines of communication leading to the bridgehead. One ship in each element was equipped with *H2X* ground-mapping radar to locate targets if they were obscured.

Allied air forces were overwhelmingly superior to the *Luftwaffe*, and succeeded in their primary aim of disrupting enemy communications and damaging airfields while allowing the flow of Allied troops into the bridgehead to continue unabated. Many crews flew more than 15 hours and went without sleep for 30 hours.

The only heavy bomber lost was a 487th BG Liberator, and two 493rd B-24s collided, as Lt Francis S. Milligan, 493rd BG, recalls:

'Our first raids, when we were flying B-24 Liberators, were pretty easy with a few exceptions, but I guess we were too green to appreciate a "milk run". We did get an early taste of war however, when, on our first mission [D-Day 6 June] we saw two of our ships collide in mid-air. The sight sobered most of us. Getting pretty badly shot up at Orleans and again at Hanover did not raise our zest for battle either.'

With the beach-head secured the uneasy marriage between the B-17 and B-24 in the 3rd BD came to an end as all five Liberator groups were converted to Fortresses. At first crews resented the changeover but they quickly grew to like the improved flying characteristics of the B-17 and praised the more spacious nose compartment and improved heating. William C. Lawson, 861st BS, 493rd BG, co-pilot in Ellis Woodward's crew, recalls:

'Our crew flew 14 missions in the B-24s. I don't believe we ever flew the same B-24 on more than two missions. The B-17 was a dream after arm wrestling a B-24 for eight months. I respected the B-24 but the Fortress, I soon learned, could withstand a lot more abuse.'

B-24 Liberators of the 44th BG, 14th CBW *en route* to Saarbrucken, Germany late in 1944. B-24 42-50427/V is *Puritanical Bitch* of the 66th BS, which was salvaged on 22 March 1945. (*USAF*)

There was one serious drawback, however, as Francis Milligan explains:

'Changing over to B-17s was practically a guarantee from the 8th AF that from now on we would be visiting the Reichland – definitely the Big League. Bremen, Merseburg, Magdeburg, Ludwigshaven, Munster, and other German cities, became our targets.'

During July the 486th and 487th BGs, 92nd Combat Bomb Wing (CBW), were removed from combat and by the end of the month were ready to begin combat operations with the B-17. Between August and mid-September the 34th, 490th and 493rd BGs, 93rd CBW also changed to the Fortress. The now surplus B-24H/Js were given to the 2nd BD groups to replace heavy losses sustained in the large number of missions flown in the months preceding D-Day.

Liberators as transports

On 28 August 20th Wing groups changed to a transportation role to fly in urgently needed fuel and supplies. From 29 August through 9 September the 93rd, 446th and 448th Groups flew 'trucking' missions, as they were called, and when the Allies launched Operation *Market Garden* using British and American airborne divisions against German-held Dutch towns on the Rhine, the Liberators were again called upon to supplement the troop-carriers. British troops landed at Arnhem and American forces at Eindhoven and Nijmegen in an attempt to secure a foothold on the east bank of the Rhine. It was planned to cut off the German Army in the Belgian sector and save the bridges and the port of Antwerp for the advancing ground forces. The Liberators' involvement was crucial.

Fuel for the Allied armour and transport was in short supply. The 458th began 'trucking' operations on 12 September, delivering just over 13,000 gallons of fuel to units in France. On 17 September the 14th and 20th Wings flew practice 'trucking' missions over Norfolk. That night motor trucks brought supplies to the bases in the region and men loaded each Liberator with about 6,000 lb of perishables and fuel supplies. Altogether, 252 supply-carrying B-24s took off for France on the first full

Divisional 'trucking' mission on 18 September, including six specially modified 458th Liberators, delivering over 9,000 gallons of fuel to General Patton's forces. In 13 days of flying in September, the 458th delivered 727,160 gallons of fuel to France.

On 27 September 315 Liberators, including 37 from the 445th, set out to bomb the Henschel engine and vehicle assembly plants at Kassel. Low cloud dogged the mission and visibility was poor. The 445th, using the *Gee* navigation beacon system, made a miscalculation at the IP and headed for Göttingen, about 30 miles north-east of Kassel. They dropped their bombs through solid cloud and then swung farther to the east, placing them well behind the main force, and headed directly into an area where the *Luftwaffe* was forming for an attack.

Ten minutes later, a few miles from Eisenach, more than 100 enemy fighters swooped down in lines of three abreast. Exploiting the clouds to excellent advantage, Fw 190s appeared at six o'clock and opened fire immediately, followed by two *Gruppen* of Bf-109s, some flying ten abreast. In minutes, 25 burning Liberators fell from the sky. Many others received serious damage. The sky seemed to be raining parachutes. Even the intervention by P-51 Mustangs of the 361st FG was not enough to save the 445th although, in a brief battle, they did shoot down several German fighters. Two B-24s crash-landed in France, a third managed to cross the Channel only to crash in Kent, while a fourth crashed near Tibenham. Only seven aircraft made it back to the airfield and they carried one dead crewman and 13 wounded.

After the withdrawal of the 492nd BG following heavy losses, the 491st BG, late of the 45th CBW, moved to take its place at North Pickenham. The same fate that befell the 492nd seemed to envelop the 491st. On 25 November they lost 16 Liberators in almost as many minutes on a mission to the Misburg oil refineries. The other 45th CBW group, the 489th, transferred to the 20th CBW.

The 2nd BD now totalled 13 groups and remained at that strength until November 1944 when the 489th was rotated Stateside for redeployment to the Pacific as a B-29 group.

Battle of the Bulge

With the German breakthrough in the Ardennes on 16 December 1944 missions intensified in support of the Battle of the Bulge. East Anglia was still in the grip of a particularly bleak December and it was not until Christmas Eve that the fog lifted sufficiently for the 8th AF to

B-24H 42-95203 *Red Ass* of the 704th BS, 446th BG, the 'Bungay Buckaroos', is seen *en route* to bomb Hanau airfield in Germany on 10 November 1944. *Red Ass* was chosen by the CO of the 446th BG, Col Jacob J. Brogger, as his lead ship on D-Day 6 June 1944, but air force public relations renamed the Liberator *The Buckaroo*. (*via Alan Hague*)

Pink and olive drab B-24Ds and Js of the 376th BG 'Liberandos', 9th Bomber Command, low over the Adriatic. (*USAF*)

mount its long awaited strike. A record 2,034 bombers, including war-weary hacks and even assembly ships, took off on the largest single strike flown by the Allied Air Forces of the war. A smaller force was dispatched on Christmas Day but such was the urgency of the situation that another raid was ordered for 29 December. Runways were covered with ice and snow, and fog added to the treacherous conditions. Despite, this Command decided that the mission in support of General Patton's forces near Metz must go ahead. At Rackheath the 467th got four Liberators off on instruments. One Liberator touched a tree on take-off and managed to land at nearby Attlebridge. Another crew baled out after heading their bomber out to sea while the other two crashed, one on top of the other.

Strategic missions and supplies

On New Year's Day 1945 the 2nd BD was redesignated the 2nd Air Division (AD) and the Liberators returned to the strategic offensive with a raid on Koblenz. Combat missions continued, weather permitting, and then in March 1945 the Liberators were once again called upon to drop supplies, this time to Field-Marshal Montgomery's 21st Army Group crossing the Rhine at Wesel. 6,000 aircraft of all types took part in the operation and the murderous ground-fire accounted for many of the 14 Liberators that failed to return. Some 104 Liberators returned to their bases damaged in one way or another.

Throughout the remainder of March and early April Me 262 jet fighters were seen regularly by Liberator crews. Fortunately, the *Luftwaffe*'s lack of fuel and a shortage of pilots lowered the number of their interceptions. The Eighth retaliated by bombing their airfields, but only the end of the war ended their threat completely.

The end came on 25 April 1945, when the 2nd AD bombed four rail complexes surrounding Hitler's mountain retreat at Berchtesgaden. Groups then flew *Trolley* missions over Western Europe, designed to allow ground crews to witness at first hand the

OPERATIONAL HISTORY: ETO AND THE MEDITERRANEAN

destruction their Liberators had wrought. From mid-May to the end of July all 13 Liberator groups of the 2nd AD returned to America via Wales and the Azores. In all, the Division flew a total of 95,948 sorties on 493 operational missions, losing 1,458 Liberators in action withand 6,032 airmen killed. Six Presidential Unit Citations were awarded and five individuals received the Medal of Honor.

Mediterranean Liberators

In July 1942 the first Liberators in the 98th BG arrived in Palestine and were based at Ramat David near Haifa. On 1 November 1942 the 1st Provisional Group was absorbed into the 376th BG, which arrived at Lydda with its desert-pink

Liberators. By 4 November Rommel's forces had been crushed at El Alamein and the Afrika Korps were on the retreat. Gen Lewis Brereton activated the 9th AF with Brig-Gen Patrick W. Timberlake commanding 9th Bomber Command. Late in February 1943 Mediterranean Air Command was activated, along with North-west African Air Forces, consisting of RAF Eastern Air Command, Maj-Gen James Doolittle's recently created 12th AF, and other units. Gen Carl Spaatz was in overall command. On 1 August, after the first Ploesti oilfields raid, the 98th and 376th BGs were transferred from the 9th AF to the 12th AF.

Gen Henry 'Hap' Arnold now planned to split the 12th AF in two to create a Strategic Air

B-24M-1-FO 44-50443 *Lo-an-Roy* of the 451st BG, 49th Bomb Wing (BW), 15th AF, dropping bombs on the railyards at Mühldorf, Germany, 19 March 1945. *(USAF)*

This 376th BG B-24 Liberator lost part of its wing to flak over Toulon, France. (*USAF*)

B-24J-15-FO 42-52440, *Calamity Jane*, of the 727th BS, 451st BG, 15th AF, which failed to return from a raid on the Korneuburg oil refinery in Vienna on 7 February 1945. Below is a B-24J-15-FO with hand-held tail guns. (*USAF*)

Force in the Mediterranean, leaving the remaining half of the 12th as a tactical organisation. This would place parts of Austria, southern Germany and eastern Europe, previously out of range of the 8th AF in England, within easy reach. On 1 November 1943 the 15th AF was officially activated with a strength of 90 B-24s and 210 B-17s inherited from the 12th AF. Initially, the 98th, 376th and four Flying Fortress groups formed the operational element of 15th AF, based in the Foggia area. Between December 1943 and May 1944 13 new Liberator groups joined the 15th AF.

Italy-based B-24s attack

Liberators flew their first mission from Italy against the aircraft factories at Wiener-Neustadt on 1 October 1943, and over the next 18 months until the end of the war the 15th AF blasted a wide range of targets in Germany and the Occupied territories. Cities in southern Germany were raided, and targets as far away as Budapest in Hungary and Czechowicka in Poland were bombed by 15th AF heavies.

The US Strategic Air Forces in Europe had long planned to launch Operation *Argument*, a

B-24Ds of the 376th BG flying over the Alps *en route* to their target. The 15th AF flew as far north as Augsburg, Germany on bombing missions. (*USAF*)

series of co-ordinated raids by the 8th and 15th Air Forces and RAF Bomber Command, aimed at smashing the German aircraft industry. After a series of postponements caused by the weather, the raids finally began on 19 February 1944, when the first raid took place in what has become known as 'Big Week'.

On 22 February it was intended that the 15th AF would strike at the Messerschmitt plant at Regensburg while the 8th struck at other targets in the Reich including the ball-bearing plants at Schweinfurt. However, the 8th had to abort because of bad weather over England and the 15th suffered heavily as the *Luftwaffe* concentrated on the Italy-based force. At the Obertraubling assembly plant 118 B-24s bombed with good results but 14 Liberators were shot down in the process.

In April 1944 the 15th AF embarked on a campaign against enemy oil targets. Over 870 refineries, many of which had been out of reach

before the formation of the 15th, were not spared from the bombs of the B-17s and B-24s. On 5 April 1944 the 15th dispatched 236 B-24s and B-17s to transportation targets in the vicinity of the Ploesti oilfields in Romania. Although the Americans did not officially admit to starting an oil offensive, the Ploesti refineries were again bombed on 15 and 24 April when 'incidental' damage was caused. Since June 1944 the 15th AF had also been bombing railway networks in south-east Europe in support of Russian military operations in Romania.

In July, the 15th AF began 'softening up' targets in southern France in preparation for the invasion code-named *Anvil*. Marseilles, Lyon, Grenoble and Toulon all felt the weight of bombs dropped by the B-24s and B-17s.

Through the summer of 1944 Austrian aircraft manufacturing centres at Wiener-Neustadt were bombed and oil-producing

B-24s of the 464th BG, 55th BW leaving the smoking Astro-Romana oil refinery near Ploesti during an attack by 15th AF B-24s on 28 July 1944. (*USAF*)

centres, too, were attacked. By the autumn of 1944 the attacks on oil targets had assumed top priority. Vast aerial fleets of B-24s and B-17s, escorted by Mustangs and Lightnings, attacked refineries at Ploesti and bombed Budapest, Komorom, Györ and Petfurdo in Hungary. Belgrade and other cities in Yugoslavia, and Trieste, in north-eastern Italy, were also bombed.

Germans surrender in Italy

On 21 March 1945 the 15th AF dispatched 366 Liberators to the jet factory and airfield at Neuburg. The attack was carried out visually and the plant was almost completely destroyed. Three days later 271 B-24s finished off the job, destroying 25 jets on the airfield in the process. On 24 March the 15th AF bombed Berlin for the first time and by the end of the month the strategic offensive

was almost over. The biggest 15th AF operation of all occurred on 15 April when 1,235 bombers were dispatched to targets near Bologna. The end came on 25 April 1945 when missions were mounted against columns of German troops trying to escape from Italy. Their escape routes in Austria and the Brenner Pass were heavily bombed. When the Germans in Italy finally surrendered, on 2 May, the Liberator groups dropped supplies and evacuated Allied PoWs.

During 18 months of operations the 15th AF had dropped 303,842 tons of bombs on enemy targets in 12 countries, destroying almost half of all fuel production capacity in Europe. The cost was considerable. Of the 3,544 B-24s assigned, 1,756 were lost in combat. In helping to free Europe the part played by the Liberators of the 8th, 9th, 12th and 15th Air Forces cannot be overestimated.

4. Operational History: RAF Liberators

In mid-1941, the shortage of very-long-range aircraft was causing Britain grave problems at a time when the German U-boat campaign was intensifying. By September increased shipping losses prompted the Admiralty to explore the possibility of employing bombers in the war at sea. RAF Bomber Command had refused to let Coastal Command have any four-engined bombers and Coastal possessed just one Liberator squadron, No. 120, based at Nutts Corner, Northern Ireland. The Liberator was ideal for use in the mid-Atlantic. This became obvious on 22 December 1941, when a Liberator of 120 Squadron drove off an Fw 200 Condor shadowing a large convoy at sea and then, two hours later, sighted and attacked a U-boat. At 16:20 hours another Liberator took over and within three hours had forced three more U-boats to submerge. By the time fuel shortage had forced the Liberator to turn for home the U-boats had been sufficiently discouraged and the convoy was molested no further.

U-boat slaughter in US waters

In January 1942 six of Germany's largest U-boats arrived in North American waters. Within three weeks, 40 Allied ships, totalling 23,000 tons, had been sunk. American defences had still not been tightened up when Doenitz ordered all his U-boats west of the British Isles and several more lying off the Azores, to take up station on the North American and Central American seaboards. America responded by using B-24Ds of the 44th BG at Barkesdale Field and the 93rd BG at Fort Myers, Florida in anti-submarine patrols in the Gulf of Mexico and along the coast of Cuba from May to July 1942. The 44th BG was credited with the sinking of one enemy submarine and the 93rd BG three. However, in one month, May 1942, the U-boat packs sank 109 ships.

Battle of the Bay

By June there was a vast increase in U-boat sinkings in the Bay of Biscay. Coastal Command was helped by the transfer of a squadron of Whitleys and eight Liberators from Bomber Command. New-type depth-charges, filled with Torpex (30 per cent more effective than Amatol) were introduced. The fitting of the Mk XIIIQ pistol ensured detonation at 34 ft below the surface. Now U-boats could also be seen on the surface of the sea at night due to the combination of ASV radar and the Leigh Light, a 24-in, 8-million-candlepower device invented by Sqn Ldr H. de B. Leigh. The operator had to switch on the light at the last possible moment just as the ASV reading was disappearing from the radar screen because the blip, which grew clearer up to three-quarters of a mile from the target, then became merged in the general returns from the sea's surface. Once the target was trapped and held in the beam the crew could release their bombs. Liberators were fitted with Leigh Lights late in 1943.

By June 1942 Doenitz had been forced to order his U-boats to proceed submerged at all times except when recharging batteries. Morale slumped and Doenitz was forced to obtain 24

Junkers Ju 88s for operations in the Bay of Biscay. Unfortunately, the enemy had obtained an ASV Mk II set from a Hudson which had crashed in Tunisia, and by mid-September 1942 they had developed the Metox 600, capable of receiving and recording ASV transmissions from up to 30 miles. Installed in large numbers of U-boats Metox 600 enabled them to dive well before the anti-submarine aircraft sighted them. An attempt to flood the Bay of Biscay with ASV transmissions failed and by January 1943 Coastal Command aircraft had almost ceased to locate U-boats by night. Later, the accurate ASV Mk III of 10-cm wavelength replaced the ASV Mk II, which had a 1.5-m wavelength.

VLR Liberators plug the Gap

While U-boat packs were prevented from finding any rich pickings in waters 500 miles from Anglo-American air bases, Doenitz was forced to concentrate his forces in the 'Greenland Gap' and the 'Azores Gap', where Allied air patrols could not penetrate. The Allies had to close the gaps using carrier-borne or VLR land-based aircraft. In August 1942 Britain asked the RCAF if they could extend their anti-submarine and convoy protection sorties to 800 miles to help close part of the Atlantic gap, but this was not possible as the first Canadian Liberators did not arrive until April 1943. In September 120 Squadron provided a detachment of five Liberators in Iceland. These were the only VLR Liberator Is in Coastal Command. They had an operational range of 2,400 miles, while the ranges of Liberator Mk IIs and IIIs were 1,800 miles and 1,680 miles respectively. Air Vice-Marshal John C. Slessor went to Washington to speed up the supply of Liberators. Two Hudson squadrons, 59 and 224, began converting to the Liberator II and V but did not become operational until October 1942. Scottish Aviation at Prestwick made all the necessary modifications to convert the high-altitude bombers to anti-submarine aircraft. Defensive armament was largely removed and radar and British navigation equipment installed. The removal of defensive armament was later abandoned as the enemy stepped up its fighter patrols in the Bay of Biscay in the defence of its U-boat force.

During August and September, type-training exercises, circuits and landings, navigational and wireless exercises and air gunnery practice were carried out. At the end of August the squadron became operational, flying convoy escorts and going on to mount anti-submarine sweeps in the Bay of Biscay in October.

Shipping losses in the Atlantic continued to mount and in October 1942 the USAAF deployed the 330th and 409th BS of the 93rd BG to provide temporary cover. On 25 October the 330th BS began Anti-Submarine Warfare (ASW) operations at Holmsley South, Hampshire, and the 409th began operations from St Eval in Cornwall.

The RAF's 160 Squadron had already begun converting from Hudsons in August 1942 at Thorney Island, re-equipping with Liberators from 59 Squadron. By 24 October 1942 four crews were deemed fully operational and made 11 to 12-hour anti-submarine escorts for a convoy well out in the North Atlantic, landing back at St Eval, Cornwall. From then the number of sorties by day and night built up rapidly and various actions took place in the Bay of Biscay and the Channel approaches, including at least three genuine U-boat attacks without radar, which was not then fitted.

No. 86 Squadron also began receiving Liberators. It served as a training unit for 160 Squadron until February 1943, when it received its own full complement of Liberators, and in March began moving to Northern Ireland where it also flew anti-submarine patrols.

Widening campaign

Operation *Torch*, the invasion of French North Africa which took place in November 1942 placed an additional strain on Coastal Command's resources. The number of anti-submarine patrols in the Bay of Biscay and the waters around Gibraltar had to be stepped up and airfields in the West Country were improved to meet the increase in operations. St Eval was converted to take 72 aircraft while Chivenor was organised for a peak complement of 88 aircraft.

Coastal Command aircraft and the 330th BS and 409th BS on detached duty with the RAF were fully committed to Operation *Torch*. They provided long-range protection duties for the invasion fleet, scouring the Bay of Biscay for up to twelve hours at a time searching for the

Liberator I (LB-30B) AM923, of 120 Squadron, with 'Stickleback' masts and 'Yagi' nose- and wing-mounted antennas for the early ASV radar. At first, the radar antennas caused interference with the aircraft's radio transmissions. The four 20-mm Hispano cannon, which occupied part of the forward bomb bay, restricted offensive loads to four 500-lb and two 250-lb anti-submarine bombs and four Mk VII or six Mk V depth-charges. The additional weight and a take-off fuel capacity of 2,500 gallons required a very long take-off run. The last of 11 Liberator Is was phased out of Coastal Command by the end of 1943. (*via Mike Bailey*)

elusive U-boats. Despite a handful of sightings, no attacks were made. At the last minute the Royal Navy asked for more air support. Coastal Command 'borrowed' a Canadian Halifax bomber squadron and eight Liberators from the 8th AF. Only two U-boats were seen to approach the invasion convoy and two Liberators of 224 Squadron sank them. On 2 November the first convoys came within reach of air cover provided from Gibraltar. On 21 November Maj Ramsey D. Potts, 330th BS, 93rd BG, was faced with an onslaught of five Ju 88s but his gunners dispatched two and damaged a third. In late November both American squadrons, having provided excellent service over the Bay of Biscay, returned to Alconbury.

Anglo-American forces

Late in March 1943, 59 Squadron returned to Thorney Island to re-equip with Liberators for the second time. Now it was to operate the much-modified VLR Liberator V, stripped of much of its armour and armament but able to carry 2,000 gallons of fuel and eight 250-lb depth-charges. That month the 1st and 2nd American Anti-Submarine Squadrons moved to Port Lyautey in North Africa, and in June became units of the 480th Anti-Submarine Group. During June 1943, the 4th and 6th Anti-Submarine Squadrons arrived at St Eval to form the 479th ASG and begin operations in the Bay of Biscay. In August they moved to Dunkeswell, Devon where the 19th and 22nd ASSs joined them. During September and October the 479th was dispersed and their duties were taken over by three Navy Squadrons from Fleet Air Wing Seven: VB-193, VB-105 and VB-110 (VPB after October 1944).

Valuable anti-submarine aircraft had been lost to the ASW effort during Operation *Torch* when control of RAF Gibraltar was temporarily transferred from Coastal Command to the AOC in French North Africa. It was not until 8 October 1943, when an air base was established in the Azores as the result of an agreement between Great Britain and Portugal, that the

An AAF B-24 attacks a U-boat. Air Force ASW responsibilities were eventually passed to the US Navy. (*USAF*)

Gibraltar squadrons were returned. In 1944 diplomatic reasons dictated that US Navy PB4Y-ls in the Azores display RAF roundels as well as the American star-and-bar insignia.

In May 1943, 53 Squadron replaced its obsolete Whitleys with Liberators and over the next sixteen months flew patrols from Northern Ireland before moving to Iceland in September 1944. During May 1943, 59 Squadron joined them at Aldergrove. Their Liberators carried the Mk 24 American acoustic homing torpedoes which revolutionised the task of killing U-boats. The Mk 24, popularly known as 'FIDO' or 'Wandering Annie', was top secret, and at the time it was a criminal offence even to mention the weapon. It entered service in May 1943 and was found to be most effective against U-boats that had just dived. An 86 Squadron Liberator and a USN Catalina each sank a U-boat with the device on 14 May 1943.

During June 1943 No. 224 Squadron Liberators, now based at St Eval, were given extra waist guns and gunners for anti-U-boat sweeps in the Bay of Biscay. From June

The 8-million-candlepower Leigh Light installation on a Coastal Command Liberator was used to help identify and aid detection of U-boats on the surface at night. (*via Mike Bailey*)

Liberator GR.VI (B-24J) KG849/A of 160 Squadron, Coastal Command on patrol. (*D. Batchelor via Mike Bailey*)

onwards they were supplemented by ever increasing numbers of Liberators from 59 Squadron and others. In September 1943, 120 Squadron ceased anti-submarine patrols between their base in Iceland, the Westmanear Islands and The Faeroes, and reverted to convoy protection patrols in the North Atlantic just south of Cape Farewell. On 30 September they were joined by a detachment of No. 59 Squadron Liberators. In October some Liberators were fitted with rockets for attacks on U-boats which stayed on the surface to fight it out. Some B-24s were fitted with long-range tanks in the forward bomb bays, giving a total endurance of nineteen hours. A number of Mk Vs were also equipped with the 8-million-candlepower Leigh Light, mounted under the outer starboard wing. Others were fitted with sonar buoys, and were modified to carry 90 anti-tank bombs converted for use against U-boats.

During the summer of 1943 No. 311 (Czechoslovak) Squadron, based at Aldergrove, Northern Ireland had converted from Wellingtons to Liberators. On the morning of 27 December the German vessel *Alsterufer* was spotted by a Sunderland heading from the South Atlantic for Bordeaux. Canadian Sunderlands were sent to bomb the 2,729-ton ship but failed to sink her. The *Luftwaffe* and the *Kriegsmarine* failed to bring relief before 'H for How' from 311 Squadron made its attack.

The Liberator roared in at low level, raking the ship with all its machine-guns despite fierce anti-aircraft fire and small mines fired into the air which descended on parachutes. The Czech crew fired rockets and then dropped a pair of 250-lb bombs from only 600 ft. Five of the rockets found their mark and both bombs opened up the hold, killing two ratings on the mess deck who were playing chess at the time to soothe their shattered nerves. The *Alsterufer* began to burn fiercely and the crew abandoned ship. However, the vessel did not sink immediately, so two Liberators of 86 Squadron finished the job four hours later. Seventy-four survivors were later rescued and many paid grudging respect to the Czech Liberator crew, which they said had flown 'unperturbed through the heaviest barrage'.

No. 311 Squadron operated Leigh Light Liberators in the last months of the war and in June 1945 transferred to Transport Command.

Iceland Liberators

In March 1944 120 Squadron was replaced in Iceland by 86 Squadron, now equipped with the Liberator Mk VI and VIII. The Boulton Paul turret had been replaced by American turrets in the nose and tail and each contained two 0.5-in machine-guns. The wireless operator's position was now over the bomb bay and the radar operator's on the flight deck. Single 0.5-in machine-guns were mounted in each of the beam positions, although great care had to be taken not to shoot one's tail off because there was no interrupter gear. There were now two

A Coastal Command Liberator of No. 547 Squadron escorts the *Kriegsmarine* heavy cruiser *Prinz Eugen* from Copenhagen to Wilhelmshaven following the German surrender in May 1945. In 1946 the *Prinz Eugen* was used as a target in the US atomic tests at Bikini Atoll in the Pacific. (*Author's collection*)

navigators in the crew and the aircraft was fitted with various electronic navigational aids.

With the Atlantic, the Bay of Biscay and the English Channel purged of the U-boat all that remained was to accept the surrender of these small craft, crewed by brave and daring men, who at one time had almost brought Britain to her knees. Had Liberators been available in sufficient quantities during the early part of the war, the U-boat menace might have been better contained. After VE day U-boats were ordered to surface and fly a black flag in surrender.

In June 1945 the bomb bays were removed from most Coastal Command Liberators and their doors sealed. Canvas seats were installed and the aircraft were transferred to Transport Command for trooping flights to India.

Liberators in the Far East

In January 1942, 159 and 160 Squadrons reformed at Molesworth and Thurleigh respectively and were equipped with Liberator Mk IIs. At the end of January 1942, 159 Squadron's ground personnel embarked for the Far East. Its Liberators flew out via the Middle East in June but became involved in long-range bombing raids from Palestine and Egypt until September. No. 160 Squadron was given training on Liberators by 86 Squadron, and flew to Nutts Corner, Northern Ireland, in May 1942 for a short period of anti-submarine

patrols with Coastal Command before flying on to the Middle East in June. Their passage to India was halted while five Liberators provided air cover for convoys desperately needed for the relief of Malta. Bombing raids on Tobruk and other targets in the Mediterranean area followed. In January 1943 its personnel were combined with those of 159 Squadron, remaining in the Middle East, and became 178 Squadron. On 15 January 1943, 160 Squadron was reorganised in Ceylon (now Sri Lanka) as a general reconnaissance unit for patrol, shipping escort duty and long-range photo-reconnaissance missions over Sumatra and the Nicobar Islands.

In October 1942 the first 159 Squadron Liberator IIs flew to Salbani, India. Operations in the first few months were at night and normally comprised two to five aircraft flying against targets at Akyab Island, Maungdaw, Buthidaung, Schwebo and the Mandalay and Rangoon areas. Later operations extended as far as Bangkok, in missions lasting 12 or more hours. Losses were not high compared with Europe because the Japanese normally held their aircraft back from the forward airfields in Burma (now Myanmar) unless they were mounting a specific offensive. Also, a high proportion of the Liberator's flying time on operations was spent over the Bay of Bengal, safe from ground-fire. However, the chances of getting home or surviving from a crashed aircraft were slim.

Early B.Mk VI Liberators of 215 Squadron being bombed-up at an airfield in India. *Ice Cold Katie*, centre, is fitted with a Boulton Paul tail turret in the nose and braced pitot tubes. (*IWM*)

Crews numbered about seven men for night operations, including a first and second pilot. Later, flight engineers were carried in place of the second pilot, though both the second pilot and flight engineer were carried in the Liberators. This proved very unpopular with the crews, especially in view of the long distances flown. Towards the end of the Japanese campaign, additional gunners were carried on daylight operations increasing the crew to 10 or even 11. Serviceability was quite good, magneto drops and oleo legs being the main exceptions.

Keeping them flying

Most major servicing was carried out at the maintenance unit at Drigh Road, Karachi. Late Liberator models arrived from the US with many minor items of equipment missing and flight crews had to improvise. No. 159 Squadron, for instance, could not get spares for their aircraft but managed to get four to six Liberators ready for operations to Ramree and Akyab. Wg-Cdr Blackburn later took command of the squadron, and Mk VI and later Mk VIII Liberators were received. When 159 Squadron flew with AAF Liberator squadrons on operations, the Americans failed to see how the British managed to take off with such heavy loads of fuel and bombs.

On 10 May 1943, 354 Squadron formed at Drigh Road, Karachi intending to operate in the long-range photographic reconnaissance role but vulnerability of the single Liberator to enemy fighters meant a change to convoy escort and anti-submarine duty in the Bay of Bengal. The first convoy escort was carried out on 4 October 1943 from Cuttack. By the time the squadron moved to Minneriya, Ceylon for anti-submarine patrols in the Bay of Bengal, in October 1944, about 236 sorties had been carried out without the loss of a single ship from the convoys covered.

Another important part of the squadron's role was the *Maxim* anti-shipping patrols off the Arakan coast from the Mavu River to the mouth of the Irrawaddy. Liberators flew their first patrol on 11 December 1943 and continued daily without a single operational failure until 28 May 1944 when the monsoon prevented further operations. These patrols, which were of an average duration of 12 hours, were instrumental in preventing the Japanese from using large merchant vessels to supply their forces in the Arakan. They were forced to use numerous small craft, many of which were sunk or damaged. In Ceylon 354 Squadron flew 57 anti-submarine patrols over the Bay of Bengal, losing two Liberators.

Allied offensive operations began in Burma in spring 1943. With the coming of the monsoon in June the Japanese practically ceased operations. The small number of Liberators and Wellingtons available were afflicted with icing in the air and occasional cyclones on the ground. These storms were so fierce as to lift a Liberator at dispersal bodily into the air. Indian coolies had to carve out improvised landing strips from the paddy fields in the Delta region. Although the runways were often of a high standard the construction of the dispersals left much to be desired. They should have been constructed with three layers of brick but the Indians were usually satisfied with just mud and as a result crews arrived in the early morning to find most of their Liberators completely bogged down.

But operations continued despite the appalling weather, disrupting the enemy's communications to such an extent that he was forced to move the bulk of his troops and supplies at night. On 18 August 355 Squadron formed at Salbani, India, flying its first mission on the night of 19/20 November 1943, when three Liberators bombed the central railway station at Mandalay.

The Allies had decrypted Japanese radio codes. The British 'Y' service was responsible for passing on intercepted information giving the exact locations of Japanese ships to the SEAC squadrons. With this information the Liberators could sink Japanese transports almost at will.

To support Gen Slim's armies in the jungle offensive, up to 12 squadrons of RAF and American aircraft at a time would mount *Earthquake* or *Major* operations.

Bombing South-east Asia

On 27 July 1944, 356 Squadron flew its first bombing raid of the war. In August, 215 Squadron at Jessore, India converted from Wellingtons to Liberators, as did 99 Squadron in September, which meant that it could now strike at targets as far as Thailand and Malaya.

Though the Liberator was one of the finest aircraft available for Burmese operations, one drawback was the relatively small bomb load the B-24 could carry over the vast distances to a target. Over distances of 1,000–1,100 miles the maximum bomb load was only 3,000 lb. However, Wg-Cdr J. Blackburn, the CO of No. 159 Squadron between July and December 1944, experimented with improving fuel consumption, and soon increased the bomb load to 8,000 lb. Soon units throughout the Strategic Air Force followed the example. Eventually, round-trips to targets as distant as the Kra Isthmus (2,300 miles), the Malay Peninsula (2,800 miles), and the approaches to Penang harbour (3,000 miles) were made carrying vastly increased bomb loads.

Long-range mine-laying

On the night of 27 October 1944, Wg-Cdr Blackburn led 15 Liberators on a round-trip of more than 3,000 miles to mine the approaches to Penang harbour. All armour plate was removed, the planes were manned with skeleton crews to save weight, and only a rear gunner was carried. The bomb bays carried extra fuel tanks as well as six 'non-sweepable' Bakelite mines. With their full fuel load the Liberators were still 5,000 lb overweight, but no one had ever flown this far south before and the Japanese were caught completely by surprise. There were no fighters or flak and the mining operation, flown entirely over water, was carried out with an exceptional degree of navigational skill. The next day carrier-borne aircraft brought back photographic evidence of shipping sunk in the Penang approaches. This success led, on 26 November 1944, to a second mining operation by Blackburn's crews in the approaches to Penang.

By the end of March 1945 the decisive battle for central Burma had been won. Japanese reinforcements which tried to infiltrate from the west were checked by resistance groups and by a technique developed by 'Wingate's Chindits'; clandestine ground observers with radio sets calling for air strikes by RAF Liberators. At the end of April they flew crossover patrols in the Andaman Sea to prevent a Japanese naval force located at Singapore from interfering with Operation *Dracula*, the planned seaborne

A Liberator of 215 Squadron coming in to land at an airfield in India. (*IWM*)

Liberator II (LB-30) of 159 Squadron. Originally sent out from the UK in the summer of 1942, the squadron spent several months flying missions over the Mediterranean before reaching India. (*Powers*)

landings at Rangoon, though the enemy pulled out before the landings could take place. On 15 May 1945, 200 Squadron at Jessore, equipped with Liberator VIs, had been renumbered No. 8 Squadron and together with No. 160 Squadron, began making supply drops to guerrillas in Malaya and Sumatra. On 20 June 1945 the Liberators were reassigned to special training, dropping containers by parachute from low level (under 150 ft) onto a small area. Before the invasion of Malaya could take place the first atomic bombs to be used in warfare were dropped on Hiroshima and Nagasaki and on 10 August 1945 Japan sued for peace.

Four Liberator squadrons flew their final operations of the war early in August 1945. On 6 August three Liberators of 356 Squadron bombed and strafed Japanese aircraft at Benkulen. The next day Nos. 99, 159 and 355 Squadrons completed their tour of operations. Five Liberators from 159 Squadron attacked two bridges on the Siam–Burma railway. Four Liberators of 355 Squadron also bombed the railway, in the Bangkok area, after an attack on shipping off the east coast of the Kra Isthmus had to be aborted. The 'railway of death' had cost the lives of 14,000 Allied PoWs involved in its enforced construction.

On 12 August, 99 Squadron flew its final operational mission of the war when three Liberators dropped supplies to guerrillas at DZ Funnel 113, in Malaya. The Liberators then dropped badly needed food and medical supplies to thousands of emaciated Allied

53

PoWs in camps in the Far East. On 28 August, 99 and 356 Squadrons in Operation *Birdcage* dropped leaflets to PoW camps in and around Singapore. Unofficially, crews dropped all the cigarettes and clothing they could obtain. By September PoWs were being flown out almost daily to Singapore. Liberators of 159 and 355 Squadrons participated in Operation *Hunger*, the ferrying or dropping of rice to the starving population of south Burma. From September 1945 until early 1946, No. 159 Squadron dropped 1.5 million lb of rice in 486 sorties. On 15 November Nos. 8, 99 and 356 Squadrons disbanded and were followed, early in 1946 by 159 and 355 Squadrons. No. 160 Squadron flew food and mail deliveries to the Cocos Islands and performed other transport duties until June 1946 when it returned to England and began re-equipping with Lancasters.

Bomber Support

Radio countermeasures (RCM) and night leaflet operations in Europe and the Far East were an important part of the air war, but it was not until late in 1943 that the RAF decided to create its own radio countermeasures group. No. 100 Group (Bomber Support) was formed under the command of Air Cdre E. B. Addison to embrace both air and ground RCM and provide a long-range fighter offensive against German air defences. In December 1943 its HQ moved to Norfolk and on 18 January 1944 was located at Bylaugh Hall near East Dereham.

Using Halifaxes and Mosquitoes and later Fortresses and Liberators, 100 Group operations were so successful that the United States established its own RCM units in Norfolk. On 19 January 1944 the 803rd BS (Provisional) was activated at Sculthorpe, equipped with B-17s. The RAF supplied and helped to install the equipment and conducted the necessary training until mid-May, when the squadron, now redesignated the 36th BS, moved to Oulton to begin operations. By August 1944 the 36th had exchanged its Fortresses for Liberators, which were capable of carrying up to 30 jamming sets and their long range made them ideal aircraft for the task. On 14 August 1944 the 36th Squadron's 11 B-24Hs and Js and two B-17s were transferred to Cheddington, where they operated principally on daylight missions.

At Oulton, black B-24s and B-17s of No. 223 Squadron, RAF, which was formed on 23 August originally as a second *Jostle* jamming unit in 100 Group, was established. When, in mid-July 1944 the wreckage of a German rocket, thought to be a V-2, was flown to England for examination, urgent steps were taken to develop a countermeasure and *Jostle* equipment was subsequently modified to the *Big Ben* configuration. However, the wreckage in the hands of the RAE Farnborough belonged not to the V-2 but the *Wasserfall* anti-aircraft missile – a fact not realised until after the war. No. 223 Squadron was equipped with B-24s previously used by the 8th AF. Such was the enormity of the threat posed by the V-2s that crews drawn from Coastal Command Liberator

Above: Liberators saw service all over the Asian theatres of war. This example, flown by No. 160 Squadron, is seen in Ceylon. (*J. T. Moore*)

Right: A Japanese ship burns on the surface on 15 June 1945, following a successful attack by Flt Lt Borthwick and his crew of 159 Squadron. (*W. J. Jones*)

OTUs became operational after only 15 hours' flying training. Daylight patrols came to an end in October and crews began their real work, which involved night operations with Bomber Command.

Electronic warfare

Operations were of two distinct types. In the first, two or three Liberators would accompany the main bomber stream to circle above the target; the special operators used their transmitters, especially *Jostle*, to jam the enemy radar defences while the heavies in the Main Force unloaded their bombs. The majority of operations were *Window* (Chaff) spoofs, which were to confuse the enemy as to the intended target. There was a radar screen created by other aircraft patrolling in a line roughly north to south over the North Sea and France. Up to eight aircraft would emerge through this screen scattering tens of thousands of small radar-reflective strips known as *Window*. This gave German radar operators the impression that a large bomber force was heading for, say, Hamburg. Then, when the Germans were concentrating their night-fighters in that area, the real bomber force would appear through the screen and bomb a different target, perhaps

Lady X, of 159 Squadron, was named after a Hollywood movie starring Lynn Barri. (*Stanley Burgess*)

Düsseldorf. After several nights, when the Germans had become used to the first group of aircraft being a dummy raid, the drill was reversed. The real bombers would appear first and with luck be ignored by the German defences, who would instead concentrate on the second group, which in reality was a *Window* spoof. No. 100 Group sometimes went in first, sometimes last, in an attempt to cause maximum confusion to the enemy, dissipation of his resources and reduction in RAF bomber losses. In June and July 1945 Exercise *Post Mortem* proved conclusively that the countermeasures had been a great success.

The British attempted to introduce jamming devices in the Mediterranean but priority always fell to the European theatre. However, the 15th AF in Italy was well equipped with RCM before the end of the war.

While RAF Liberators in Europe often encountered strong flak defences by night, their sister squadrons in the Far East had little need for electronic countermeasures (ECM). Towards the end of the war five RAF Liberator squadrons were operating against the Japanese in daylight but the enemy was equipped with only primitive radar equipment. Nevertheless a special ELINT (electronic intelligence) flight was activated under the control of 159 Squadron. The flight, formed to monitor enemy W/T and R/T transmissions and plot his radar stations, began operations in September 1944. ELINT missions were carried out until early January 1945 when the Special Flight began dropping leaflets.

A 356 Squadron Liberator prepares to taxi in June 1945. (*C. Berry*)

A 356 Squadron Liberator flown by Flg Off Schmoyer dropping supplies to a PoW camp in Burma on 6 September 1945. (*Stanley Burgess*)

Of all the theatres of operations in which the B-24 served during World War 2, it was in the Mediterranean that it saw the most widespread and diversified service in both the RAF and the AAF. As early as December 1941 108 Squadron, then based in Egypt and equipped with Wellington bombers, received four Liberator Mk IIs, which had been originally intended for France. These unarmed Liberators remained in Egypt until it was decided that 108 Squadron should use them to convert fully from Wellingtons to Liberators. However, after they had been fitted with Boulton Paul gun turrets, the plan to convert the whole squadron to Liberators was abandoned and only two were ever used for bombing operations. Some others, which had been used for conversion training, were modified for supply-dropping duties. The four Mk IIs operated as a separate flight from the rest of 108 Squadron, which continued using Wellingtons right up to November 1942. For a time the flight operated from Palestine.

Day and night missions

The Liberators of 205 Group in the Mediterranean not only flew daylight missions in their B-24s but night missions as well. No suitable heavy night-bombers could be spared so the B-24 was chosen in spite of its many operational disadvantages for night work, principally the bright flames and white-hot turbo-supercharger exhausts which could alert enemy night-fighters. Since night-fighter activity was not as intense over Italy and southern Europe it was considered worth the gamble. Another disadvantage was the 0.50-calibre machine-guns. They had a much better range than the standard British 0.303-in guns, but as the gunner could not see far enough in the dark to avail himself of this, the only advantage was their superior hitting power. However, as soon as the gunner fired, the flash from the guns ruined his night vision so he had little chance of aiming on a second attack. The front gun turret was useless also, as was the under gun turret since the light from the turbo-chargers made it impossible to see fighters at night. The belly turret was removed and so were the guns in the front turret, which was faired over with fabric. The beam guns also were taken out when it was found that fighter attacks always came from behind.

Conversion to the Liberator was slow. On 15 January 1943 178 Squadron was formed at Shandur in the Suez Canal Zone from a detachment of 160 Squadron and began receiving Liberator Mk IIIs. The following night three Liberators took off and bombed targets in Tripoli. It was not a full-scale beginning and 178 remained the only Liberator Squadron in 205 Group until October 1944, although on 14 March 1943 a 'Special Liberator Flight' was formed at Gambut, Libya. It was later re-designated 148 Squadron and began special duties, dropping arms and supplies to Resistance groups in Albania, Greece, and Yugoslavia.

Operations over Italy

In January 1944 148 Squadron moved to Italy and when not engaged in special operations its aircraft joined with other squadrons of 205 Group on heavy bombing raids on northern Italy and southern Europe. By April 1944, the powerful Mediterranean Allied Strategic Force was playing a vital role in the conduct of the war, which was by no means confined to Italy or the Italian Front. The 15th AF continued to pound targets by day while the RAF Liberators and Wellingtons struck under the cover of darkness. In June the combined forces bombed railway networks in south-east Europe in support of Russian military operations in Romania.

Through the summer of 1944 aircraft manufacturing centres at Wiener-Neustadt in Austria were bombed day and night, as were oil-producing centres, often in conjunction with Bomber Command in England. Liberators and Wellingtons of 205 Group flew unescorted at night from their bases in southern Italy and stoked up the fires left by the American bombers during the day. Of special importance to the Germans were the Hungarian and Romanian railway systems which came under constant Allied aerial bombardment.

Gardening operations

When the Russians deprived the Germans of the use of the Lwow–Cernauti Railway the only alternative route linking Germany with the grainlands of Hungary and the oilfields of

M-Mother, an electronic warfare Liberator of 223 Squadron, 100 Group at Oulton, Norfolk in 1944. (*CONAM*)

Liberator *W for William* of 70 Squadron, 231 Wing, 205 Group, seen at the major Allied bomber base located at Foggia, Italy. (*Arthur Anderson*)

An RAF Liberator VI of the Balkan Air Force, used to support Special Operations in the region. (*IWM*)

Another mission symbol is painted on the nose of a South African Air Force Liberator VI of 31 Squadron, somewhere in Italy in 1944/5. *(Dave Becker)*

Romania was the Danube, which by mid-March 1944 was carrying more than double the amount carried by rail. Even a temporary halt in this river traffic would seriously hamper the German war effort and in April 1944 No. 205 Group began *Gardening* operations, sowing the waterways with mines. On the night of 8 April three Liberators and 19 Wellingtons of 178 Squadron dropped 40 mines near Belgrade. Over the next nine days 137 more mines were dropped and in May the total number dropped had risen to over 500. No *Gardening* sorties were flown during June but on the night of 1 July 16 Liberators and 53 Wellingtons dropped 192 mines in the biggest operation of the campaign. The following night another 60 mines were dropped.

Early *Gardening* sorties were only flown on nights of the full moon, as the aircraft had to fly below 200 ft. Sorties continued in July, August and September. On the night of 4 October, four Liberators and 18 Wellingtons flew the final mission of the operation and dropped 58 mines in the Danube in Hungary west of Budapest, north of Györ, and east of Esztergom.

In six months of operations, 1,382 mines were laid by Liberators and Wellingtons of 205 Group in 18 attacks. The effect on the supply route was catastrophic. Several ships were sunk and blocked the waterway in parts. By May, coal traffic had virtually ceased. Canals and ports were choked with barges and by August 1944 volumes of material transported along the Danube had been reduced by about 70 per cent.

Covert operations

In June 1944 the Balkan Air Force, which included one flight of Liberators, had been formed to supply partisan groups in Yugoslavia. The Balkan Air Force flew more than 11,500 sorties into Yugoslavia and delivered over 16,400 gross tons of supplies to the partisans while 2,500 people were flown in and 19,000 brought out of the country. In England, between August and October 1943, three Liberators were used on covert trips to Poland, but these long trips were fraught with danger so it was decided to operate SOE aircraft from the Mediterranean theatre. No. 1575 Flight (which became 624 Squadron in 1943), 1586 Flight (which became 301 Pomeranian–Polish Squadron in November 1944) and 148 Squadron (which, with four Liberators had been supplying Resistance groups in Albania, Greece, and Yugoslavia since May 1942) were based in North Africa. By 1944 airfields in Italy were used on occasion. The aircraft operated in the Balkans, Czechoslovakia, southern France and, towards the end of the war, Austria and Germany, dropping spies, resistance leaders, arms, and supplies.

In August 1944 the advancing Red Army was approaching Warsaw. The Polish Home Army under General Bor was persuaded to rise against the German occupiers. The Soviets made no attempt to support the rising and when Gen Bor requested all possible air support the Russians refused RAF and American supply aircraft permission to make emergency landings in Soviet territory. The Special Duty squadrons in England were fully committed to *Overlord* so the task of supplying the Polish Home Army was given to the Mediterranean Allied Air Forces. Despite fears that the flights were suicidal, the Polish situation became so acute that a trial sortie involving a few aircraft of 1586 (Polish) Special

An SAAF B.Mk VI Liberator sets off on a mission over Italy in 1944. (*Dave Becker*)

Duty Flight was made. This proved successful and two Liberator squadrons, 31 (SAAF) and 178, of 205 Group, were diverted from the invasion of southern France to support them.

On the five nights between 12 and 17 August, 17 of the 93 aircraft dispatched failed to return. The South Africans lost eight Liberators in four nights. Operations ceased but they were restarted with aircraft from 1586 Flight after protests from the Polish authorities. Four of the nine aircraft failed to return over two nights and, after further losses, bad weather prevented any further missions. In early September the Russians finally agreed to co-operate but by then the Polish, RAF, and SAAF units had lost 31 aircraft out of 181 dispatched in 22 nights of operations.

Island bombing

Meanwhile the Liberators of the 15th AF and 178 Squadron continued pounding isolated enemy garrisons all over the Mediterranean area. No. 178 Squadron had operated Liberators since the beginning of 1943 and had built up an impressive record, listing among its targets Crete, the Aegean Islands, and the Ploesti oil refinery. Apart from a few

scattered units employing a handful of Liberators, 178 was the only true RAF B-24 squadron in the Mediterranean up to October 1944. But in that month 37 Squadron, based at Tortorella, began exchanging its Wellingtons for the Liberator Mk VI and three more Wellington squadrons were to follow. In January 1945 70 Squadron at Tortorella began re-equipping with Mk VIs, as did 104 Squadron at Foggia Main, a month later. In March, 40 Squadron at Foggia Main also began converting to Liberator VIs.

The Wellington pilots discovered that the B-24 flight deck was roomier than the 'Wimpy' and it had a superb radio and auto-pilot. Crews soon got used to the performance and they enjoyed the Liberator's superior stability and comfort. The tricycle undercarriage, which no British front-line bomber had at the time, was vastly superior to tail-wheel designs, giving greater all-round visibility and ease of handling on the ground.

The B-24 did not have the standard British blind-flying panel. Instead, the instruments were arranged rather haphazardly and checks for take-off and landing were only possible by having the flight engineer read out from a long

V-Victor of No. 37 Squadron was badly damaged by one of six 1,000-lb bombs dropped by *R-Roger* during a raid on the Monfalcone shipyards in northern Italy on 16 March 1945. Despite losing the port inner propeller and suffering damage to the forward fuselage, Flt Lt Lionel Saxby, the pilot, succeeded in getting *V-Victor* back 300 miles to their base at Tortorella. Incredibly, no-one was killed, though pieces of engine entered the back of wireless operator Cliff Hurst. Even though the bomb smashed a 6 ft x 4 ft hole near the mid-upper turret, the gunner, Wally Lewis, was uninjured. Hurst made a full recovery and was awarded the DFM. (*Ken Westrope*)

check-list. The auxiliary engine-driven generator, used amongst other things to provide enough electricity to run the hydraulic brake pressure pumps, removed the constant anxiety of losing brake power when taxiing. This had been a major worry on the Wellington, due to the slow-running engines not being able to maintain pressure.

No. 205 Group now operated six Liberator squadrons, two of which were South African. On 25 April 1945 61 Liberator bombers, and seven Pathfinder (PFF) Liberators of No. 614 Squadron attacked the Freilassing marshalling yards four miles north-west of Salzburg in the last bombing raid of the war. VI or 'Victory in Italy' Day was announced on 6 May.

For a few days after the German surrender, Liberators transported petrol and supplies to the British 8th Army advancing from northern Italy into Austria, and they also flew British troops from Italy to Athens to help suppress a Communist rising. Over the next few months the squadrons left Italy, one by one. On 6 November 148 Squadron flew to Gianacalis, Egypt and on the 13th 178 Squadron moved to Fayid, where in December they disbanded. Crews were posted to 70 Squadron, 205 Group at Shallufa. Trooping continued until February 1946, when Lancasters replaced the Liberators. The American bombers were returned to the USA since there were now sufficient British aircraft available for all tasks.

5. Accomplishments: The Liberator Men

During World War 2, B-24 crewmen served with several air forces in every theatre of war. Stories of their heroism and bravery under fire are legion. Nine individuals were awarded the Medal of Honor, five of them posthumously.

The first Liberator MoH was awarded for an action on 6 July 1943, during the Battle of the Solomon Islands, to Lt-Cdr Bruce Van Voorhis. Voorhis, the CO of VP-102, took off with his crew on the 700-mile flight for the Japanese-held Greenwich Island. Alone and in total darkness, their mission was to prevent a surprise enemy attack on American forces. Despite treacherous and varying winds, limited visibility and difficult terrain, the crew got through to their target, a seaplane tender off Kapingamarangi (a small atoll north-west of the Solomons). In spite of overwhelming aerial opposition, Van Voorhis and his gallant crew executed six low-level attacks, destroying the Japanese radio station, anti-aircraft guns and other installations with bombs and machine-gun fire. Voorhis's gunners destroyed one Japanese fighter in the air and another three on the ground. Caught in his own bomb blast, Van Voorhis and his crew crashed into the lagoon off the beach and perished. For his sacrifice and lone fight against the odds Lt-Cdr Van Voorhis was posthumously awarded the MoH.

Ploesti, on 1 August 1943, was the only mission for which five airmen were awarded America's highest military honour – three of them posthumously. The same month the only Liberator Victoria Cross was awarded. On 11

Flg Off Lloyd Allan Trigg VC. (*via C. Bowyer*)

August 1943, Liberator BZB32 *D-Dog* of 200 Squadron, based at Bathurst (now Banjul) in Gambia, was on anti-submarine patrol off the coast of West Africa. Its pilot, Flg Off Lloyd Trigg of the Royal New Zealand Air Force, sighted *U-468* on the surface about 240 miles south-west of Dakar. The Type VIIC U-boat,

Lt-Col Leon R. Vance (left) with his 489th BG CO, Col Ezekiel Napier. (*USAF*)

commanded by *Oberleutnant-sur-See* Clemens Schamong, was returning to La Pallice, France, after a war cruise in the Atlantic. Trigg attacked immediately. Schamong elected to remain on the surface and fight it out, using the U-boat's powerful Flakvierling quadruple 20-mm cannon. Two 20-mm shells hit the Liberator in the centre section, and the plane was on fire in several places when it arrived in a position to attack. Trigg could have broken off, but as he flew over the vessel at just 50 ft he released a stick of six depth charges to be released. Two exploded just 6 ft from the U-boat's hull, and within twenty minutes *U-468* was sinking beneath the waves. However, the stricken *D-Dog* perished with her, a victim of the submarine's anti-aircraft fire, and Trigg and his gallant crew died. About 20 German sailors managed to climb to safety,

but sharks killed several others and soon only Schamong and six others remained. They all clambered into one of the Liberator's dinghies, which had floated clear after being released by the impact of the plane hitting the sea, and were picked up. Their account of the action resulted in a posthumous award to Trigg of the Victoria Cross, Britain's highest military decoration, on 2 November 1943.

Leon Vance: Medal of Honor

On 5 June 1944 the 8th Air Force attacked coastal defence installations, three 'Noball' (V-1 launcher) sites and a railway bridge in France. One of six Liberators lost was *Missouri Sue*, a 65th BS, 44th BG pathfinder ship that carried the 498th BG deputy commander, Lt-Col Leon R. Vance. A malfunction prevented bomb release at the target, a V-1 site near Wimereaux, and despite protests, Vance ordered the crew to go around again. This time the bomb drop was made by hand, but two bombs hung up. An 88-mm salvo burst directly under the port wing, putting three engines out of action, instantly killing pilot Capt Louis A. Mazure and seriously wounding Earl L. Carper, the co-pilot.

Vance, who was standing behind the pilot's seats, had his right foot virtually severed but despite this he managed to reach the controls to feather the three dead engines. Carper cut all four engines and turned *Missouri Sue* towards England. Vance managed to get into the pilot's seat and succeeded in ditching the aircraft off Broadstairs, Kent. The impact blew him clear, and he was quickly picked up by an air-sea rescue unit who gave him immediate medical attention. His right foot was amputated and he was later invalided home in a medical evacuation C-54, but somewhere between Iceland and Newfoundland the Skymaster, with its crew and patients, disappeared without trace. Vance was the fifth and last 2nd Bomb Division (BD) airman to be awarded the MoH.

During the oil campaign, Lt Donald D. Puckett, a pilot in the 98th BG 'Pyramiders', brought B-24J-35-CO 42-73346 back from Ploesti on 9 July 1944 against incredible odds. Just after 'bombs away', flak peppered the Liberator, killing one crewmember and severely wounding six others. Puckett handed over to his co-pilot while he inspected the B-24, calmed

Liberators of the 718th BS, 449th BG, 15th AF in formation amid flak. (*USAF*)

the crew and cared for the wounded. Two engines had been put out of action, the control cables had been cut, the oxygen system set on fire and the bomb bay was awash with fuel and hydraulic fluid.

Puckett succeeded in hand-cranking open the doors, allowing the fuel to drain away, and he ditched the guns and equipment to save weight, but the Liberator still seemed doomed. Puckett ordered the crew to bale out, but three refused to do so and he would not leave them. He fought hard to pull the B-24J out of its fatal descent, but it crashed into a mountainside and exploded. Puckett was posthumously awarded the MoH for giving his life unhesitatingly and with supreme sacrifice, in his courageous attempt to save the lives of three others. It was the last of seven Medals of Honor awarded for raids on Ploesti.

For his actions in the South China Sea on the night of 25/26 October 1944, Maj Horace C. Carswell Jr. in the 308th BG was awarded the Medal of Honor. Carswell piloted a B-24 in a one-plane strike against a Japanese convoy of 12 ships with at least two destroyer escorts. He took them completely by surprise and made one bombing run at 600 ft, scoring a near miss on one warship and escaping without drawing fire. He circled and, fully realising that the convoy was thoroughly alerted and would meet his next attack with a barrage of anti-aircraft fire, began a second low-level run, which resulted in direct hits on a large tanker.

A hail of steel from Japanese guns riddled the Liberator, knocking out two engines, damaging a third, crippling the hydraulic system, puncturing one fuel tank, ripping uncounted holes in the aircraft and wounding the co-pilot. But by a magnificent display of flying skill, Carswell controlled the B-24's plunge towards the sea and he carefully forced it into a halting climb in the direction of the

Chinese coast. On reaching land, where it would have been possible to abandon the staggering bomber, one of the crew discovered that his parachute had been ripped by flak and was therefore useless. Maj Carswell, hoping to cross mountainous terrain and reach an airfield, continued onwards until the third engine failed. He ordered the crew to bale out while he struggled to maintain altitude, and refusing to save himself, chose to remain with his comrade and attempt a crash-landing. He died when the B-24 struck a mountainside and burned.

Fighter attacks

Every day and most nights until final victory B-24 crewmen braved the enemy, the elements, and the unexpected. Men like 24-year-old S/Sgt Henry A. DeKeyser, waist gunner, 576th BS, 392nd BG, 14th CBW, 2nd AD, flew every mission of their tour on Liberators. DeKeyser, who flew 35 missions (plus two uncredited and six aborted) between 7 June and 23 December 1944, recalls the dangers:

'Whenever any German fighters attacked us they made head-on or dead astern attacks. As a waist gunner most of the times I had just a split second to fire my 50-caliber gun, getting off at best two or three rounds, and they were gone. But from the nose or the tail turrets we could get off two or three bursts. You never took the time to see if you had done them any damage as you were to busy searching the sky for the next attack. We never had time to think much under fighter attack, but flak was another story. When you could fire your .50 it gave you a feeling of being able to do something, but with flak you felt completely helpless, and unable to protect yourself, so you just prayed, trusted in God and sweated bullets, as the saying goes. In other words you were scared silly. We had flak suits to wear, which were hung over your shoulders front and back, and if you were in a turret you sat on a thick piece of armour plate. The weight of the suit wasn't too bad, but when you had to stand up in the waist position, the weight of the suit pressed the bottoms of your feet flat and you soon had a real aching back and feet. You also had to have the help of one of your crewmates to get the flak suit on, and we never got into them until the formation was almost ready to cross the mainland coast.'

Few ever forgot their first mission. John Rickey, 578th BS, 392nd BG, was a gunner in the B-24 42-100117, *G.I. Jane*, piloted by Captain Neele Young. Rickey recalls:

'Our first mission was to Bremen, Germany, in December 1943, with 22 bombers. Ten enemy fighters were encountered, but no losses on either side. Four of our planes were damaged by flak. I can't remember any one specific mission that was the worst, but I do remember one where an airplane flying on our right wing received a direct flak hit or one of their bombs went off prematurely. It caused him to go down and did a lot of damage to our *G.I. Jane* plane. It severed a control cable to the tail turret hydraulic pump and twisted the tail turret around so that I couldn't get out. But they cranked it around by hand and I went forward to the flight deck for the rest of the mission. Another time my flying suit shorted out and my socks caught on fire. That was some sight, seeing me come out of my turret tearing off my boots and socks and beating out my smouldering socks. Most harrowing experience was landing a B-24 Liberator with the ball turret down and the ball gunner still in it. My pilot called the tower for instructions on what to do. They told him to get the rest of the crew ready to bail out. Better to lose one man instead of ten. He called back and told them he thinks he can land the plane only if he has the rest of the crew in the front of the plane and bring it in on the nose. Luckily that's what he did. It took the ground crew two hours after we landed to get the ball gunner out.'

Some missions were more memorable than others. For John W. Butler, left waist gunner, 328th BS, 93rd BG, the mission to Frankfurt on 4 February 1944 in 42-99949 *Naughty Nan* was one he would never forget.

'At 21,000ft the temperature was -54°, which is very cold. Before we passed the enemy coast my heated boots went out. I went up on the flight deck to borrow the radioman's, as on the flight deck they had heat. We ran into heavy flak twice on the way to the target. Over the target it was pretty damn good. You should have seen Carey and I throwing the tin foil out. It was supposed to spoil the German

Maj-Gen George E. Stratemeyer talks with 39-year old West Pointer Col Leon Johnson, CO of the 44th BG, (centre), Maj Howard 'Pappy' Moore and Lt Bob Brown of the 67th BS, by the nose of B-24D-5-CO 41-23817 *Suzy Q*, at Shipdham on 21 April 1943. In the background is B-24D-25-CO 41-24278 *Miss Delores*, which FTR (failed to return) with Lt Brown and his crew on the disastrous mission to Kiel, 14 May 1943. Brown was among the survivors who became PoWs. Johnson, who led the 'Flying Eightballs' in *Suzy Q* on the low-level mission to 'White V' – Columbia Aquila – at Ploesti on 1 August 1943, was awarded the Medal of Honor for his leadership on the raid. The medal was presented to him in a ceremony at Shipdham on 22 November 1943, by which time he commanded the 14th CBW. (*USAF*)

radar equipment. We dropped our bombs and started for home. My heated suit went out for good. I had the ball-turret gunner came back in the waist to take my place as I then went up on the flight deck to try and keep warm. Our bombardier lost his oxygen supply so he came up on the flight deck also. My feet were frozen. The radioman fired a red flare as we came into land and the meat wagon followed us down the runway. They took us all to hospital. There were around twenty fellows in the hospital with frostbite. This was the worst mission I was

on to have so many things go wrong.'

The cold was unbearable at altitude, as Maj Ralph H. Elliott, 467th BG, 8th AF pilot confirms:

'In winter flying, we wore nylon inner gloves, then a wool pair, and finally a leather pair over that. I think the gunners had mittens with a separate trigger-finger, but if a gun jammed, they'd take them off to work on it. If they took off the liners too, at 40 below zero their fingers would freeze to the gun. If they froze bad enough, the gunners would end up

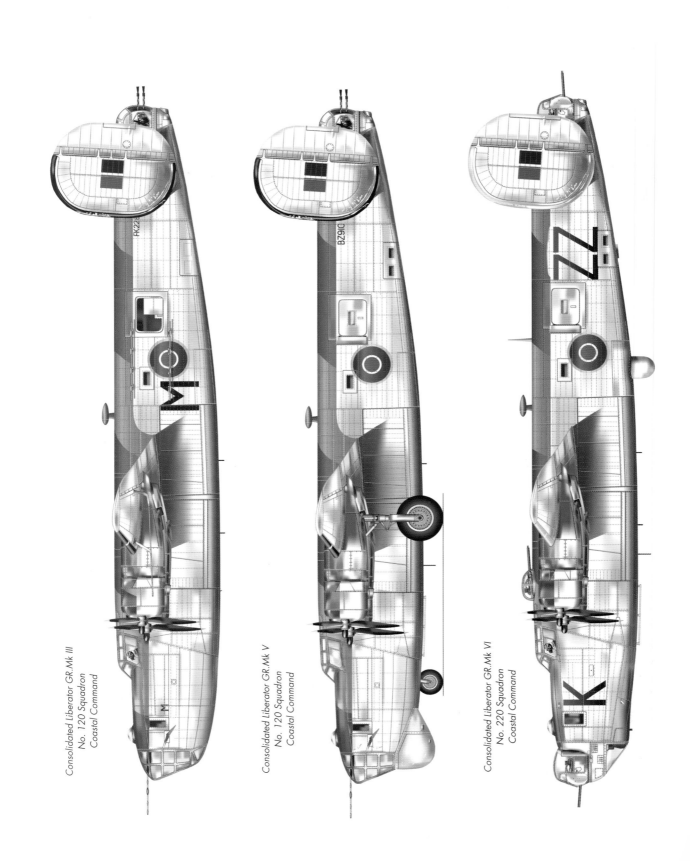

*Consolidated Liberator GR.Mk III
No. 120 Squadron
Coastal Command*

*Consolidated Liberator GR.Mk V
No. 120 Squadron
Coastal Command*

*Consolidated Liberator GR.Mk VI
No. 220 Squadron
Coastal Command*

Consolidated Liberator Mk VIII
in the colours of No. 99 Squadron, India, 1945
RAF Museum, Cosford

Consolidated Liberator B-24D-5-CO
44th Bombardment Group
67th Bombardment Squadron

Consolidated Liberator B24D-165-CO
93rd Bombardment Group

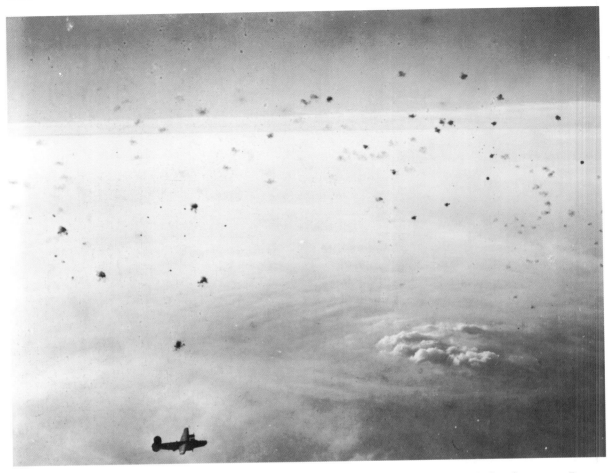

B-24s of the 392nd BG, 8th AF approach their target on 10 August 1943. High-altitude bombing over Europe was dangerous. Fighters could be deadly, but at least you could shoot back at them. There was no way of shooting back at the dirty black bursts of anti-aircraft artillery, and you just had to pray that none of shells being loaded into the *Luftwaffe* flak guns below had your Liberator's name on it. (*USAF*)

with gangrene and lose the fingers. I saw my first case of dry gangrene in the States, where a man had frozen his fingers on a training mission. The outer joints of all of his fingers were black, and the doctors had to decide whether to amputate or just let them fall off.'

As if the elements were not enough, flak was a major threat – many crews feared the black bursts more than the enemy fighters, and the *Luftwaffe* was a respected adversary. The firepower of the German fighters could, when brought to bear against mass formations of bombers, reduce a B-24 to pieces in a few brief seconds, as this combat report by Oskar Romm,

IV. *Sturm*/JG3 Udet, confirms:

'Just like during my first downing of a four-engine bomber over Oschersleben, 7 July 1944, my approach for the attack was divided into three actions, [coming in quick succession]. First, to fire into the fuselage to hit the machine-gun positions, then hit the pilot's compartment, and finally to hit and set fire to two engines on one side of the aircraft. If two engines on one side were on fire, aeronautical control over the plane was almost immediately [lost]. I first attacked the bomber on the left position of the flight, then the one on the right and lastly the leading B-24 of the flight. I then pulled up in a

Members of an 863rd BS crew undergo post-mission interrogation on the hardstand at Debach following the 493rd BG mission on 19 July 1944. Left to right, they are: Lt Abraham 'Hap' Galfunt, co-pilot; Lt Shelton, intelligence officer; Lt P. B. Slawter, navigator; Lt Chenard, intelligence officer; Capt Payne, intelligence officer; Lt R. R. Harding, bombardier; Lt S. A. Abraham, pilot. (*Galfunt*)

steep turn and, while flying over them, observed them going down, spinning, burning, and the breaking off of wings in the area of the burning engines. The film from my gun cameras showed the downing, demonstrating in an appalling way the location of the hits and the effect of the shots on the three aircraft. The two MK 108 30-mm guns did the most devastating damage. I opened up aerial combat by first firing the two 13-mm machine-guns, then the two 20-mm guns, and between less than 400 meters and ramming distance with all six guns firing off short bursts.'

In the Pacific there was the added danger of long overwater flights and Japanese fighter pilots' fanatical disregard for their own lives. An incident on 10 May 1944 mission to Dublon Town, Truk Atoll by the 308th BG is not only a testament to this fanaticism but it also reveals how strong the Liberator was, even though usually it could not be easily ditched. The bombing altitude was 19,000 ft and the pattern was good. Prior to the bomb run, 15 to 20 Japanese fighters were seen but no attacks were made until the turn away from the target. The attack then began and it lasted for 30 minutes. Lt Willock's B-24D was hit by a Tojo fighter trying to dive through the formation. It

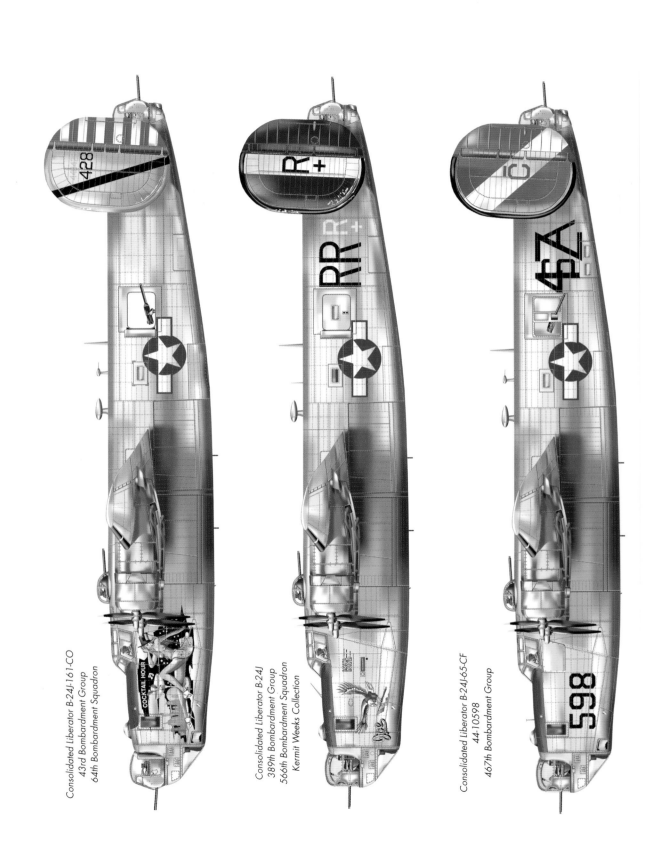

Consolidated Liberator B-24J-161-CO
43rd Bombardment Group
64th Bombardment Squadron

Consolidated Liberator B-24J
389th Bombardment Group
566th Bombardment Squadron
Kermit Weeks Collection

Consolidated Liberator B-24J-65-CF
44-10598
467th Bombardment Group

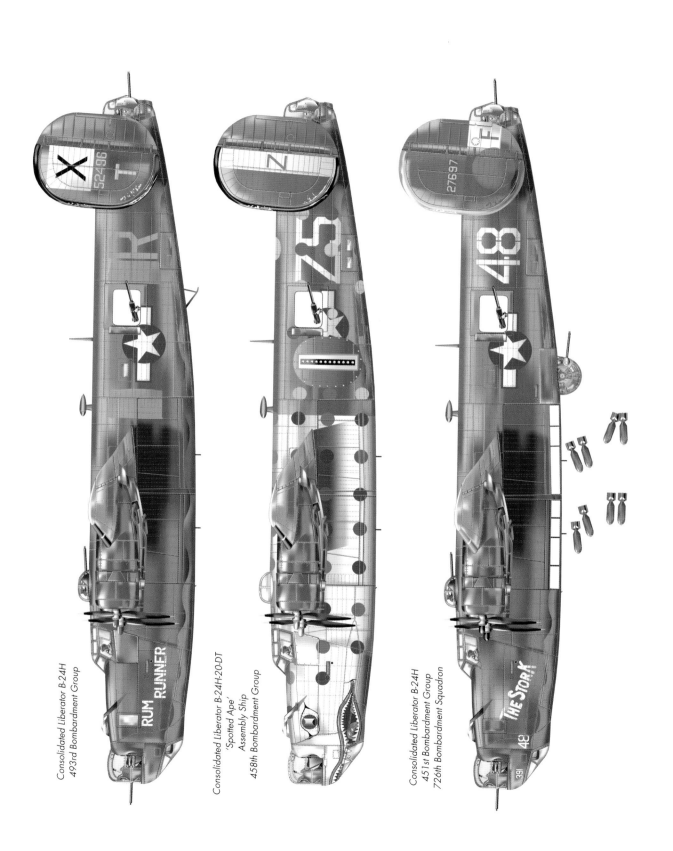

Consolidated Liberator B-24H
493rd Bombardment Group

Consolidated Liberator B-24H-20-DT
'Spotted Ape'
Assembly Ship
458th Bombardment Group

Consolidated Liberator B-24H
451st Bombardment Group
726th Bombardment Squadron

B-24 Ball-turret gunner Rock Daigle. (*Daigle*)

crashed into the bomber, whose tail turret sheared off. Part of the left vertical stabiliser and all but a quarter of the horizontal stabiliser were destroyed. As a result of the damage, the B-24D went into a tight spiralling dive to the right and dropped from 19,000 ft to 12,000.

Rock J. Daigle, ball-turret gunner, 370th BS, in *Old 085* piloted by Lt H. Surbaugh, adds:

'The fighter hit the B-24 tail after being shot at by top turrets – maybe it was the intention of the pilot to crash into the B-24 or maybe he meant to go through the formation and misjudged. Plane parts tumbled through the air just after impact. The Tojo's wings fluttered down and the entire empennage was intact. I didn't see the tail portion of the B-24 or its tail-turret, which fell off with the gunner still in it. Off to the side and lower down was the fighter pilot's parachute with the pilot dangling below the canopy. One other B-24 crewman said that he was headless. Some Japanese pilots had static lines attached to their chutes in case they get thrown out while unconscious. This may have been the case here, and the impact may have severed the pilot's head.'

Willock and his co-pilot gained control of

the disabled B-24 and headed back to base. Everything that could be thrown out was, and the pilot was able to maintain a speed of 150 mph and an altitude of 6,000 ft. However, a weather front was encountered and with only 100 gallons of fuel remaining, a water landing was made and the crew took to their dinghies. Only three of the crew were still alive when the USS *Hutchins* arrived to pick up survivors the next day, 11 May 1944.

Terror and trauma

T/Sgt Forrest S. Clark, a gunner in the 67th BS, 44th BG, 8th AF, concludes:

'I have many impressions of the most fearsome parts of flying in B-24s. Among the most frightening were those few minutes when we were over the target area and on the bomb run. Those were minutes of pure terror and trauma that could make you sweat right through the heated suit or flak jacket. Nothing is as pure fearful as those gut-wrenching minutes. At first I used to look down when I was flying in the radio operator position and when the bomb bay doors were open I could see all the way to the target miles below. But I soon got over that habit and I didn't bother to look down anymore. I held on for dear life, beads of sweat inside my flight gloves and a trickle down my back. We seemed to hang there, suspended in a kind of sky jelly, an aspic of air, vulnerable to the 100th degree, merely a huge hunk of metal hanging almost motionless, so it seemed, for the flak gunners and fighters to get a dead bead on and to blow us to hell. On major targets like Munster, or Berlin, the suspense of those minutes was totally and emotionally draining. I would then hear the steady click, click as the bombs released from their racks and pray that none got hung up and all would go earthward. I also prayed those damn bomb bay doors would not creep as they sometimes did on 24s. I would have to get up and grab the manual door handle to hold them back and steady to stop the creep if the automatic didn't work. Then the cry, "Let's get the hell out of here" and off we would go trying to scramble to regain the formation if we could. Sometimes we did and sometimes not. The next mission we would have to do it all over.'

Gathering a formation of 50 or more heavy bombers took time. To ease the process, the 8th AF used brightly coloured formation ships, usually war-weary veterans without armament or heavy equipment, on which the aircraft flying on a mission formed up. After the bomb group or combat wing was in position, the formation ship headed homeward while the other aircraft set off on their mission. (*USAF*)

Early B-24s were painted olive drab all over. Later in the war American bombers were usually flown in natural metal finish, which saved weight and reduced drag. (*USAF*)

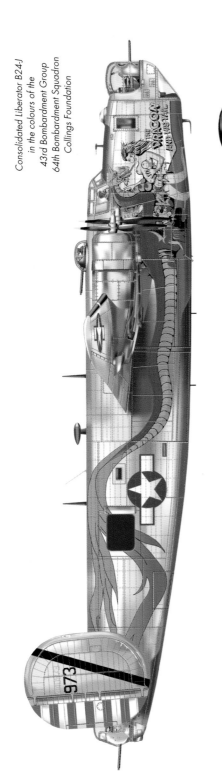

Consolidated Liberator B24-J
in the colours of the
43rd Bombardment Group
64th Bombardment Squadron
Collings Foundation

Consolidated Liberator B24-J-145-CO
Assembly Ship
491st Bombardment Group

Consolidated Liberator B24-M
392nd Bombardment Group
(These markings applied to B-24M on display at the
American Air Museum, Duxford)

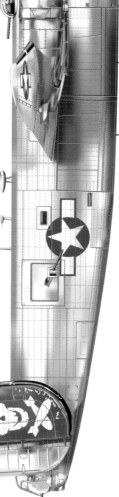

*Consolidated Liberator B24-M-11-FO
Pathfinder Aircraft
446th Bombardment Group
704th Bombardment Squadron*

*Consolidated Liberator B24-M-35-CO
90th Bombardment Group
321st Bombardment Squadron*

*Consolidated Liberator LB-30A (YB-24)
Transatlantic Ferry Transport*

A B-24 of the 489th BG, 8th AF over the Schulau oil refinery on 6 August 1944. (*USAF*)

USAAF and USN B-24 Medal of Honor Awards
1943–44

DATE	RECIPIENT	UNIT	MISSION
6 July 1943	Lt-Cdr Bruce Avery Van Voorhis*	VP-102, USN	Battle of the Solomons
1 August 1943	Lt-Col Addison E. Baker*	93rd BG, 8th AF	Ploesti, Romania
1 August 1943	2/Lt Lloyd D. Hughes*	389th BG, 8th AF	Ploesti, Romania
1 August 1943	Maj John L. Jerstad*	93rd BG, 8th AF	Ploesti, Romania
1 August 1943	Col Leon W. Johnson	44th BG, 8th AF	Ploesti, Romania
1 August 1943	Col John R. Kane	98th BG, 9th AF	Ploesti, Romania
5 June 1944	Lt-Col Leon R. Vance Jr.	489th BG, 8th AF	Wimereaux, France Killed 26 July near Iceland
9 July 1944	1/Lt Donald D. Puckett*	98th BG, 15th AF	Ploesti, Romania
26 October 1944	Maj Horace C. Carswell Jr.*	308th BG, 14th AF	South China Sea

* Posthumous

6. Liberator at War:
Other Versions and Variants

On 17 January 1941 the first LB-30A for the RAF (AM258) made its maiden flight, and the first production models began flying over the Atlantic in March that year. Six YB-24s, identical to the original XB-24 except for the removal of wing slots and the addition of de-icers, were diverted for service as LB-30A transports on the new Trans-Atlantic Return Ferry Service route between Montreal, Newfoundland and Prestwick, in Scotland, a distance of 3,000 miles. The seventh YB-24 had armour and self-sealing fuel tanks and was accepted by the AAC in May 1941.

Atlantic crossings

At first the LB-30As were flown by BOAC crews, and later by the RAF Ferry Command pilots. The transports enabled increasingly large numbers of American-built aircraft to be collected and flown to Britain for combat with the RAF. Many VIPs and service and civilian personnel made the Atlantic crossing in these unarmed transport Liberators, which were designated LB-30A (equivalent to Liberator I). Later examples designated LB-30B (equivalent to Liberator II) were also operated on the transatlantic route. Their tasks included flying ferry pilots to Canada to collect and fly home American-built aircraft for the RAF and to transport VIPs to their destinations.

The first LB-30 arrived in the UK on 14 March 1941, to be used by British Overseas Airways Corporation (BOAC). Three crashes in August and September cost 54 lives but the service was considered highly successful. The surviving aircraft eventually served in the civil markings of BOAC. The first westbound Liberator left Prestwick on 14 May 1941.

After the defeat of France in June 1940 Britain took over the French LB-30 contract, specifying 165 aircraft (139 Liberator IIs, six LB-30As and 20 Liberator Is) with self-sealing fuel tanks, armour and power-operated turrets. Turbo-superchargers, essential for boosting power at altitude, were not installed. By December 1941 65 LB-30s had been delivered, and six YB-24s and 20 VLR (very-long-range) B-24As were diverted from the AAF to the RAF.

Liberator II AL504, which was issued to 511 Squadron, served as Prime Minister Winston Churchill's personal transport from October 1942 to June 1944, before being rebuilt by Consolidated with a stretched forward fuselage and single tail. It was re-issued to 231 Squadron and went missing on a flight between the Azores and Ottawa on 26 March 1945. The B-24As, whose delivery began on 29 March 1941, went to 120 Squadron in RAF Coastal Command at Nutts Corner, Northern Ireland, as the Liberator I (LB-30B). No. 120 Squadron had previously been operating the Short Sunderland, which had a range of 1,300 miles but the Liberator increased the range to 2,400 miles. Eventually, 22 squadrons would operate the Liberator in Coastal Command.

Equipment installed in Britain included the centimetric ASV (Air-to-Surface-Vessel) Mk II radar installation, which had both forward- and sideways-looking antennas. These Liberators entered service in September 1941. The ASV

BOAC LB-30A of the Return Ferry service approaching Ailsa Craig during an Atlantic flight to Prestwick. (*IWM*)

was tested in the US, and in August 1941 was adopted for service use as the SCR-521. An improved microwave version, ASV-10 (SCR-517), was developed and housed in a chin radome on Liberator II AL507, which was flown to Britain in March 1942, where it joined 120 Squadron. AL507 was joined later by AL593, a second 'Dumbo', a nickname acquired because of the chin housing. AL507 operated later with 224 and 59 squadrons and in August 1944 transferred to BOAC, operating as G-AHYC. It was damaged beyond repair in a landing accident on 13 November 1948.

The Liberator II, built under the LB-30 contract, was the first model with a longer nose. Commercial R-1830-S3C4-G engines and Curtiss (instead of the usual Hamilton) propellers were installed. Provision was made for two power-operated gun turrets and it was armed with 14 0.303-in Browning machine-guns, installed in the UK. Four were contained in the Boulton Paul top turret, four in the tail turret, two in each waist position, one at the tunnel hatch and another in the nose. The first LB-30 crashed on a test flight on 2 June 1941, but 139 more were built, and deliveries to the

RAF began on 8 August. Originally these were intended for bomber squadrons in the Middle East, but when the US entered the war in December 1941, 75 LB-30s were taken over by the AAF, the last in January 1942.

In June 1942 the Liberator bomber entered RAF service. Eight .50-calibre guns could be installed, including two hand-operated tail guns, single guns in the nose, waist and tunnel positions, and two in a Martin power-operated turret, when available, located amidships.

Liberator III

In RAF service the B-24D became the Liberator III. Its engine carried turbo-superchargers which gave much-improved high-altitude performance. 366 Liberator IIIs were supplied under direct British contracts. Nineteen B-24Ds had already been supplied to the Royal Canadian Air Force in September 1943, while 12 others went to the Royal Australian Air Force in 1944. RCAF Liberators were similar to the RAF Mk II, but in the RAF version a Boulton Paul turret fitted with four 0.303-in machine-guns usually replaced the Consolidated tail turret. The Liberator IIIA and subsequent versions were

C-109 'Flying Tankers' operated by Air Transport Command lining up for take-off from an Indian base. They were used to ferry fuel to B-29 bases in the China–Burma–India theatre. C-109s were converted B-24J and B-24L aircraft with the turrets deleted and with specially designed fuel tanks in the bomb bay and in the nose, giving a total fuel capacity of 2,900 US gallons. (*USAF*)

supplied under Lend-Lease and handed over to the RAF by the AAF.

A later-series B-24D was designated the Liberator Mk V, equipped with additional fuel tanks in wing bays and ASV radar either in a retractable radome in the ventral position aft of the bomb-bays or in the 'Dumbo', or chin position. The fitting of long-range tanks, however, in both Mks II and III Liberators proved to be a slow process and this adversely affected the supply of these desperately needed aircraft. The installation of the ASV Mk III also took time.

By February 1943, a few Liberators in 224 Squadron were equipped with the American-designed ASV Mk IV. The Liberator I, which was armed with four 20-mm fixed cannon in trays under the fuselage and six British Browning 0.303-in guns (two of them an opening in the tail), could carry up to eight 250-lb depth charges on 16-hour patrols.

Altogether, Britain received 366 B-24Ds as the Liberator III, and GR.Mk V for Coastal Command, while Australia received 12, and Canada 19. Britain also received eight B-24Gs and 22 B-24Hs (Liberator VI). Beginning in November 1943 deliveries of the B.Mk VI and GR.Mk VI Liberators to the RAF began. These versions were Convair-built B-24J models with American turrets. Some VIs used the Boulton Paul tail turret but most were equipped with Consolidated or Motor Products turrets.

In all, the RAF received 1,157 B-24Js. The GR.Mk VI anti-submarine aircraft later incorporated a radome containing centimetric radar in place of the ball turret. The B.Mk VI was used overseas and by the RCAF for training. Australia received 145 B-24J models, and Canada acquired 49.

In the Middle East the Liberator VI operated mainly against Axis shipping in the Mediterranean. Thirty-six Mk VIIIs (B-24Ls) began operation late in 1944. Each was equipped with centimetric radar designed for PFF operations against ground targets. In the Far East the Mk VI was the principal bomber used in the final Burma campaign ending with the capture of Rangoon.

By the end of the war 2,445 Liberators had been delivered to Britain from America, 2,070 of them under Lend-Lease arrangements. Of the Lend-Lease total, 1,865 Liberators were bombers, while there were 24 C-87 (Mk VII) and 26 RY-3 (C.Mk IX) transports. The C.IX saw service with No. 45 Group, Transport Command on routes between Canada and SEAC across the Pacific in the closing stages of the war. A further 55 B-24s were transferred to the RAF and RAAF from the AAF. All of these were in addition to the 112 LB-30As, Mk Is and IIs received prior to the agreement.

C-87 transport

Because of its very-long-range capability and spacious fuselage, the Liberator was adapted for a transport role in the AAF, the Navy and the RAF. Altogether, 276 C-87 transport variants, developed from the B-24A and based on the B-24D, were delivered from Fort Worth to the AAC, beginning on 14 December 1942. The first transports were converted B-24Ds from the Fort Worth production lines. Accommodation was increased to 25 passengers and five crew, and windows were fitted along the fuselage. All turrets were deleted, although some were armed with four .50-calibre machine-guns for 'Hump' operations in China. Some 24 C-87 (Liberator C.VII) models were allocated under Lend-Lease and they served in No. 46 Group, Transport Command in England and No. 229 Group in India.

In US service the C-87 was used early in the war by the Air Corps Ferrying Command. The designation C-87A was applied to transport Liberators equipped with ten berths to be used as executive sleepers. Six were built in 1943 and had uprated Twin Wasp engines. An armed variant, the C-87B, was never proceeded with. Neither was the C-87C projected transport variant of the single-finned B-24N.

Other wartime conversions made to the basic Liberator airframe included the C-109 flying tanker, the F-7 photo-reconnaissance aircraft, and the AT-22 flying classroom. All told, 200 B-24s were converted as aerial tankers to support B-29 groups based in the CBI theatre, while in January 1943 a B-24D was converted to an XF-7 photographic aircraft with 11 cameras. Some 213 conversions of later B-24 models followed, to F-7, F-7A and F-7B reconnaissance aircraft for use in the Pacific. Five AT-22s were manufactured to train flight engineers.

Anvil Project

The *Anvil* project to use PB4Y-1 'drones' packed with explosive and launch them against German installations arose from the enthusiasm of Admiral King, who placed USN experience of radio-controlled drones at the Army's disposal. The Navy had experimented with remotely controlled drones since 1937. *Aphrodite* was a similar project jointly proposed by the AAC.

C-87 Liberator Express 44-52987, built at Convair Fort Worth. Some 276 C-87s were built, beginning in September 1942. The first transports were converted B-24Ds from the Fort Worth production lines. (*General Dynamics*)

US Ambassador to the Soviet Union, William Averell Harriman, arriving at Berlin–Templehof in a C-87A for the Potsdam Conference in mid-July 1945. (*Ken Armstrong*)

In mid-1944 the belief that there were four V-2 sites in the Pas de Calais – at Mimoyecques, Siracourt, Watten, and Wizernes – ready to rain V-2 rockets on London, gave the *Anvil* project added urgency. Early in July the first *Anvil* Liberator was modified as a drone at the Naval Air Material Center in Philadelphia, where two Lockheed PV-1 Venturas were also modified as 'mother' aircraft. A control system and an arming panel were installed in the PB4Y-1s. All non-essential equipment, such as the co-pilot's seat and bomb racks, was removed. The aircraft was gutted and new supports were installed to shore up the fuselage to take the additional weight. The PB4Y-1 had the advantage over the B-17 in being able to carry a bigger explosive load. It could carry 12 crates of Torpex, 12 times the load of a V-1.

The *Aphrodite* and *Anvil* bombers were to be flown by two-man crews who would bale out over England and the rest of the flight would be taken over by 'mother' aircraft whose operators would guide the drones to their targets by remote control. The method chosen utilised a television camera installed in the nose of the drone and a receiver set in the controlling aircraft. This enabled the controllers to view the approach of the target as if they were in the nose of the drone itself. Controlling the drone and arming the explosives once the crew had baled out were effected by means of radio signals from the mother aircraft.

Among the crews of the SAU-1 (Special Attack Unit), as the Navy termed it, was Cdr James A. Smith, who commanded the project,

his executive officer, Lt Wilford 'Bud' Willy, a pilot and a leading expert on radio control, and volunteers from VB-110, including 29-year-old Lt Joe Kennedy Jr., son of the former US Ambassador to Britain, Joseph P. Kennedy. *Aphrodite* and *Anvil* personnel began work at Fersfield, Suffolk under the overall control of the 3rd BD. Logistic support was provided by the 388th BG at Knettishall, nearby.

At first, test flights with simulated loads were made. The first *Aphrodite* mission went ahead on 4 August. Two of the B-17s were shot down and the other two crashed and exploded, one after the crew had baled out. On 6 August two more drones left Fersfield. One crashed into the Channel and the other exploded just after the crew baled out over East Anglia. The USN tried to mount the first *Anvil* mission on 11 August. Ten tons of Torpex and six demolition charges, each containing 113 lb of TNT, were distributed throughout the PB4Y-1 but this mission was cancelled because of fog.

Death of a Kennedy

Joe Kennedy and 'Bud' Willy flew the Navy's first mission on 12 August, to the secret weapon site at Mimoyecques. Unfortunately, their PB4Y-1 was ripped apart by two explosions 1,500 ft over Saxmundham before they had a chance to bale out. Stunned crews circled the burning wreckage, which had spread over a wide area of the countryside, damaging over 150 houses in a half-mile radius, but they could do nothing. Kennedy and Willy were later decorated and Joseph S. Kennedy Snr. received

Liberator II transport AL547 operated with 511 Squadron between October 1942 and June 1944. In December 1944 AL547 was transferred to BOAC, operating as G-AGKU. (*Scottish Aviation*)

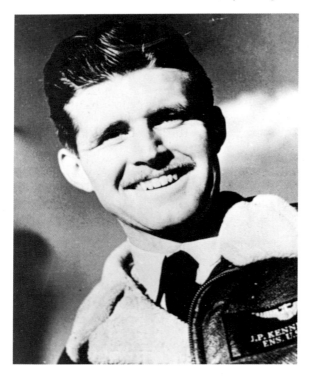

Lt Joseph P. Kennedy Jr. (*USN*)

the Navy Cross on his son's behalf. A report on the crash was prepared and one of its recommendations was that a second PB4Y-1 drone be employed immediately against the enemy but the Allied ground forces soon overran Normandy and captured the rocket-launching sites. It was decided, therefore, that the second Navy drone should be flown against submarine pens on the island of Heligoland. The mission took place on 3 September 1944 and Lt Ralph D. Spalding successfully took off from Fersfield and baled out through the nose-wheel hatch after manually arming the drone. It was then guided to Heligoland by a 'mother' ship but missed the submarine pens. For his efforts Spalding was awarded the Navy Cross. He was killed on 14 January 1945 in an air crash in North Africa on his way back to the United States. Spalding's mission was the last the Navy flew. The Air Force continued operations until New Year's Day 1944 but of the 17 Air Force missions and two Navy missions, none of the drones hit the target

PB4Y-2 Privateer

In April 1943 Convair and the USN decided to begin production of a new patrol bomber, the

Above and right: Former RAAF C-87 VH-EAI, after being transferred to Qantas Empire Airways. (*Author's collection*)

PB4Y-2 Privateer, based on the B-24. On 3 May Convair allocated three PB4Y-ls (B-24B) for conversion to XPB4Y-2. The wings and tricycle landing gear were retained but more fuel, guns and radar were added and the fuselage was stretched by 7 ft to 74 ft to accommodate the new electronics (and two electronics operators). More powerful R-1830-94 Twin Wasp engines were used but since patrol planes operate at low altitudes, the turbo-superchargers were deleted to produce a higher sea-level speed.

A new single fin replaced the twin-tailed empennage of the B-24 and this improved stability. A Martin A-3 dorsal turret complemented the mid-upper turret, making six turrets in all, while a second 0.50-in machine-gun was installed in each of the tear-shaped Engineering Research Company (ERCO) side blisters, making twelve .50-calibre guns in total. The ball turret was deleted.

The XPB4Y-2 made its first flight on 20 September 1943, and on 15 October a production contract was placed for 660 Privateers. Deliveries began in March 1944. A further contract, for 710 PB4Y-2s, was placed on 19 December 1944, but most were cancelled and by October 1945, when production ceased, a total of 740 of these large patrol aircraft had been built. A number of USN Liberators were modified for reconnaissance duties as PB4Y-1Ps and these served until as late as 1951, being redesignated in their last year as P4Y-lPs.

The 801st (P) Group (later 492nd BG) was activated at Harrington, Northants, in the summer of 1943 using crews and B-24D Liberators from the disbanded 479th Anti-Submarine Group at Dunkeswell, Devon. The Liberators received a series of modifications to enable the crews to fly so-called *Carpetbagger* missions at night to occupied Europe, where they dropped supplies and agents, or Joes, to the underground armies in France and the Low Countries.

Late in the war these missions were extended to include Scandinavia when a team headed by Bernt Balchen, the famous Arctic explorer, mounted *Sonnie* operations from Leuchars in Scotland. In total, 3,016 passengers were evacuated, including 965 American internees.

Carpetbagger operations

For *Carpetbagger* operations the B-24s were painted black overall and the ball turret was deleted. The ball-turret opening became the

On 6 November 1944 *Carpetbagger* B-24-20-CF 42-63980 *Playmate* was flown by Maj Bestow 'Rudy' Rudolph, 858th BS, to New Delhi, India, and China with OSS representatives to investigate the possibilities of mounting *Carpetbagger* operations in the CBI (China–Burma–India) theatre. Seen here at Myitkyina, Burma, *Playmate* was one of the oldest Liberators in the group, having served in the 567th BS, 389th BG as *Missouri Mauler* before flying 89 *Carpetbagger* missions. It was ideal for demonstrating the modifications needed for covert operations over enemy territory. (*Bestow Rudolph*)

'Joe-Hole' through which agents were dropped by parachute. Late B-24 models had their nose turret removed and replaced by a 'greenhouse' which permitted the bombardier an excellent view of the drop zone so he could assist the navigator with spotting landmarks. Suppressors, or flame dampers, were fitted to the engine exhausts and the two waist guns were removed. Only the top- and tail-turrets were retained. Oxygen equipment was removed because of the low altitude flown, and a variety of special navigational equipment and radar was installed.

While the OSS (Office of Strategic Services) directed operations and handled the reception grounds in the occupied countries, the Carpetbaggers themselves came under Special Operations, 8th AF. *Carpetbagger* missions contributed hugely to the success of the invasion of Normandy in the run up to D-Day. In June 1944 the 801st BG flew no less than 424 sorties, of which 347 were successful. A further 397 sorties were flown in July.

When the final *Carpetbagger* mission was flown on 16 April 1945, a total of 82 agents had been parachuted into Germany by aircraft of the Dijon mission set up in France. In all operations to France, the Low Countries and Scandinavia, 26 aircraft and 208 crewmen were lost in action.

Appendix 1
Weapons

Boulton Paul rear turret installation containing four 0.303-in Browning machine-guns fitted to a Coastal Command Liberator. (*IWM*)

Coastal Command Liberator III (B-24D) FL927 armed with side-mounted rocket rails. (*via Mike Bailey*)

Sperry ball-turret installation on an RAF GR.VI Liberator in India. (*IWM*)

Convair tail turret mounted in the nose position of B-24D *The Green Hornet* of the 7th BG at Funafuti Island, Ellice Group, in April 1943. (*USAF*)

The cramped waist-gun positions on early-production B-24 models were soon improved using staggered guns and ammunition belts, which replaced the drum magazines for the machine-guns. (*USAF*)

0.50-in Colt Browning machine-guns installed in the tail position of an RAF Liberator II of 108 Squadron at Fayid, Egypt. (*IWM*)

A beam gunner (waist gunner) manning a Colt Browning M.2 .50-calibre gun on an RAF Coastal Command Liberator. Note the flash eliminator on the muzzle and the wind deflector in the open position forward of the waist hatch. (*IWM*)

A B-24L-15-FO with Emerson nose turret. The navigator's window was bulged as the turret obscured his forward visibility. Ford produced 1,250 B-24Ls at Willow Run beginning in August 1944. (*USAF*)

A Martin A-3 dorsal turret with two .50-in machine guns mounted on an RAF Liberator B.VI. The hatch on left is for dinghy stowage. (*Burgess*)

Sgt G. W. S. Challen of 108 Squadron in a 'home-made' tail turret on Liberator Mk II LB-30 AL574 at Fayid, Egypt. The twin .30s are mounted on a tripod. Sliding doors were added later. (*via Mike Bailey*)

A hydraulically operated Motor Products A-6B turret (an improved version of the Consolidated turret) seen on an RAF Liberator. The turret was used in the nose and the tail of late-model Liberators. (*via Mike Bailey*)

Appendix 2
B-24 Production

MODEL	No. BUILT	PLANT(S)
LB-30A	6	Consolidated Aircraft Corp San Diego CA
Liberator I	20	Consolidated Aircraft Corp San Diego CA
Liberator II	140	Consolidated Aircraft Corp San Diego CA
XB-24	1	Consolidated Aircraft Corp San Diego CA
YB-24	6	Consolidated Aircraft Corp San Diego CA
RB-24(YB-24)	1	Consolidated Aircraft Corp San Diego CA
B-24A	120	Consolidated Aircraft Corp San Diego CA
RB-24A	9	Consolidated Aircraft Corp San Diego CA
RB-24C	9	Consolidated Aircraft Corp San Diego CA
B-24D	2381	Consolidated Aircraft Corp San Diego CA
	305	Convair Fort Worth TX
	10	Douglas Tulsa OK
B-24E	490	Ford Motor Co Willow Run MI
	144	Convair Fort Worth TX
	167	Douglas Tulsa OK
		R-1830-43 engines
XB-24F	(1)	Converted from B-24D for testing thermal de-icing system
B-24G	430	North American Aviation Dallas TX
		R-1830-43/-65 engines
B-24H	1780	Ford Motor Co Willow Run MI
	738	Convair Fort Worth TX
	582	Douglas Tulsa OK
B-24J	2792	Consolidated Aircraft San Diego
	1587	Ford Motor Co Willow Run MI
	1558	Convair Fort Worth TX
	205	Douglas Tulsa OK
	536	North American Aviation Dallas TX
XB-24K	(1)	Single-finned version modified by Ford from B-24D
B-24L	1250	Ford Motor Co Willow Run MI

MODEL	No. BUILT	PLANT(S)
	417	Consolidated San Diego CA
RB-24L/TB-24L	(1)	B-24L conversion for B-29 training
B-24M	1677	Ford Motor Co Willow Run MI
	916	Consolidated San Diego CA
XB-24N	(1)	B-24J converted to single tail
YB-24N	7	Ford Motor Co Willow Run MI
B-24N		Orders for 5,168 cancelled
XB-24P	(1)	B-24L converted by Sperry for fire control research
XB-24Q	(1)	B-24L converted by GEI for radar-controlled turret-tests
C-87	278	Consolidated San Diego CA Liberator Express transport version of B-24D
C-87A	6	Consolidated San Diego CA. 3 for USN and 3 for AAF
XC-109	(1)	Converted by Ford from B-24E to fuel tanker
C-109	(208)	B-24Js & Ls converted to C-109 tankers
AT-22/TB-24D	(5)	Converted C-87s for flight engineer training
XF-7 (B-24D)	(1)	Cvtd at Lowry AB, Colorado to PR to include 11 cameras in nose, bomb bay and tail
F-7 (B-24D)	(4)	Cvtd by Lockheed at Northwest Modification Center, St Paul, Minneapolis, MN
F-7A (B-24H/J)	(89)	Cvtd; 3 cameras in nose and 3 vertical cameras in aft bomb bay
F-7B	(124)	122 B-24J/2 B-24M conversions. Six cameras located in aft bomb bay
Liberator Ferret	(173)	B-24D and 172 B-24Js converted for passive Ferret mission
XB-41	(1)	B-2D converted for bomber escort
PB4Y-1	977	Consolidated San Diego CA USN B-24D
PB4Y-2	736	Consolidated San Diego CA USN single-finned version
RY-1/2	(8)	C-87/C-87A transport conversion
RY-3	39	PB4Y-2 transport version
R2Y	2	Liberator Liner

MODEL	SERIAL NOS.	NO. BUILT	MODEL	SERIAL NOS.	NO. BUILT	MODEL	SERIAL NOS.	NO. BUILT
LIBERATOR II (CO)	AL503/AL641	139	C-87 (CF)	41-11704	1	C-87 (CF)	41-23791/23793	3
LB-30A (CO)	AM258/AM263	6	C-87 (CF)	41-11705	1	B-24D-5-CO	41-23794/23824	31
LIBERATOR I (CO)	AM910/AM929	20	C-87 (CF)	41-11706/11709	4	B-24D-7-CO	41-23825/23849	25
LIBERATOR II (CO)	FP685	1	B-24D (CO)	41-11710/11727	18	B-24D-7-CO	41-23853/23858	6
XB-24 (CO)	39-680	1	B-24D (CF)	41-11728/11733	6	C-87 (CF)	41-23859/23862	4
YB-24 (CO)	40-696/701	6	B-24D (CO)	41-11734/11741	8	C-87A (CF)	41-23863	1
B-24D (CO)	40-2349/2368	20	C-87 (CF)	41-11742/11747	6	B-24D-10-CO	41-23864/23902	29
B-24A (CO)	40-2369/2377	9	C-87 (CF)	41-11748/11753	6	C-87 (CF)	41-23903/23905	3
B-24C (CO)	40-2378/2386	9	B-24D (DT)	41-11754/11756	3	B-24D-10-CO	41-23906/23919	14
B-24D (CO)	41-1087/1142	56	B-24D (CO)	41-11757/11787	31	B-24D-13-CO	41-23920/23958	39
B-24D-CO-1	41-23640/23668	29	C-87 (CF)	41-11788/11789	2	C-87 (CF)	41-23959	1
B-24D-CO-1	41-23671/23693	23	B-24D (CO)	41-11790/11799	10	B-24D-13-CO	41-23960/23969	10
B-24D (CO)	41-11587	1	C-87 (CF)	41-11800	1	B-24D-15-CO	41-23970/24003	34
B-24D (CF)	41-11588/11589	2	B-24D (CO)	41-11801/11836	36	C-87 (CF)	41-24004/24006	3
B-24D (CO)	41-11590/11603	14	C-87 (CF)	41-11837/11838	2	B-24D-15-CO	41-24007/24026	20
B-24D (CF)	41-11604/11605	2	B-24D (CO)	41-11839/11863	25	C-87 (CF)	41-24027/24029	3
B-24D (CO)	41-11606	1	B-24D (DT)	41-11864	1	B-24D-15-CO	41-24030/24099	70
B-24D (CF)	41-11607	1	B-24D (CO)	41-11865/11906	42	B-24D-20-CO	41-24100/24138	39
C-87 (CF)	41-11608	1	C-87 (CF)	41-11907/11908	2	C-87 (CF)	41-24139/24141	3
B-24D (CO)	41-11609/11626	18	B-24D (CO)	41-11909/11938	30	B-24D-20-CO	41-24142/24157	16
B-24D (CF)	41-11627/11628	2	B-24D (CO)	41-23640/23668	29	C-87 (CF)	41-24158	1
B-24D (CF)	41-11629/11638	10	C-87 (CF)	41-23669/23670	2	C-87A (CF)	41-24159	1
B-24D (CO)	41-11639/11642	4	B-24D (CO)	41-23671/23693	23	C-87 (CF)	41-24160/24163	4
B-24D (CF)	41-11643/11654	12	C-87 (CF)	41-23694/23696	3	B-24D-CO-20	41-24164/24171	8
B-24D (CF)	41-11655/11657	3	B-24D-1-CO	41-23697/23724	28	C-87 (CF)	41-24172/24173	2
B-24D (CO)	41-11658/11673	16	B-24D-1-DT	41-23725/23727	3	C-87A (CF)	41-24174	1
B-24D (CO)	41-11674/11676	3	B-24D-1-CO	41-23728/23755	28	B-24D-20-CO	41-24175/24219	45
B-24D (CF)	41-11674/11676	3	B-24D-5-DT	41-23756/23758	3	B-24D-25-CO	41-24220/24311	92
B-24D (CO)	41-11677/11703	27	B-24D-5-CO	41-23759/23790	32	B-24D-25-CO	41-24339	1

MODEL	SERIAL NOS.	NO. BUILT	MODEL	SERIAL NOS.	NO. BUILT	MODEL	SERIAL NOS.	NO. BUILT
B-24E-1-DT	41-28409/28416	8	B-24D-10-CF	42-63837/63896	60	B 24J 30-CF	44-10253/10302	50
B-24E-10-DT	41-28417/28444	28	B-24D-15-CF	42-63897/63971	75	B-24J-35-CF	44-10303/10352	50
B-24E-15-DT	41-28445/28476	32	B-24D-20-CF	42-63972/64046	75	B-24J-40-CF	44-10353/10374	22
B-24E-20-DT	41-28477/28500	24	B-24J-1-CF	42-64047/64141	95	B-24J-45-CF	44-10375/10402	28
B-24E-25-DT	41-28501/28573	73	B-24J-5-CF	42-64142/64236	95	B-24J-50-CF	44-10403/10452	50
B-24H-1-DT	41-28574/28639	66	B-24J-10-CF	42-64237/64328	92	B-24J-55-CF	44-10453/10502	50
B-24H-5-DT	41-28640/28668	29	B-24J-12-CF	42-64329	1	B-24J 60-CF	44-10503/10552	50
B-24H-10-DT	41-28669/28752	84	B-24J-10-CF	42-64330/64346	17	B-24J-65-CF	44-10553/1 0602	50
B-24H-15-DT	41-28753/28941	189	B-24J-15-CF	42-64347/64394	48	B-24J-70-CF	44-10603/10652	50
B-24H-20-DT	41-28942/29006	65	B-24E-25-CF	42-64395/64431	37	B-24J-75-CF	44-10653/10702	50
B-24E-DT	41-29007/29008	2	B-24H-10-CF	42-64452/64501	50	B-24J-80-CF	44-10703/10752	50
B-24E-10-CF	41-29009/29023	15	B-24D-155-CO	42-72765/72814	50	B-24J-30-NT	44-28061/28276	216
B-24E-15-CF	41-29024/29042	19	B-24D-160-CO	42-72815/72864	50	C-87 (CF)	44-39198/39298	101
B-24E-20-CF	41-29043/29061	19	B-24D-165-CO	42-72865/72914	50	B-24J-145-CO	44-40049/40148	100
B-24E-25-CF	41-29062/29115	54	B-24D-170-CO	42-72915/72963	49	B-24J-150-CO	44-40149/40248	100
B-24H-1-CF	41-29116/29187	72	B-24J-1-CO	42-72964/73014	51	B-24J-155-CO	44-40249/40348	100
B-24H-5-CF	41-29188/29258	71	B-24J-5-CO	42-73015/73064	50	B-24J-160-CO	44-40349/40448	100
B-24H-20-CF	41-29607/29608	2	B-24J-10-CO	42-73065/73114	50	B-24J-165-CO	44-40449/40548	100
B-24E-1-FO	42-6976/7005	30	B-24J-15-CO	42-73115/73164	50	B-24J-170-CO	44-40549/40648	100
B-24E 5-FO	42-7006/7065	60	B-24J-20-CO	42-73165/73214	50	B-24J-175-CO	44-40649/40748	100
B-24E-10-FO	42-7066/7122	57	B-24J-25-CO	42-73215/73264	50	B-24J-180-CO	44-40749/40848	100
B-24E-15-FO	42-7123/7171	49	B-24J-30-CO	42-73265/73314	50	B-24J-185-CO	44-40849/40948	100
B-24E-20-FO	42-7172/7229	58	B-24J-35-CO	42-73315/73364	50	B-24J-190-CO	44-40949/41048	100
B-24E-25-FO	42-7230/7464	235	B-24J-40-CO	42-73365/73414	50	B-24J 195-CO	44-41049/41148	100
B-24H-1-FO	42-7465/7717	253	B-24J-45-CO	42-73415/73464	50	B-24J-200-CO	44-41149/41248	100
B-24H-5-FO	42-7718/7769	52	B-24J-50-CO	42-73465/73514	50	B-24J 205-CO	44-41249/41348	100
B-24E (FO)	42-7770	1	B-24G (NT)	42-78045/78069	25	B-24J-210-CO	44-41349/41389	41
B-24D-30-CO	42-40058/40137	80	B24G-1-NT	42-78070/78074	5	B-24L-1-CO	44-41390/41448	59
B-24D-35-CO	42-40138/40217	80	B-24G-5-NT	42-78075/78154	80	B-24L-5-CO	44-41449/41548	100
B-24D-40-CO	42-40218/40257	40	B-24G-10-NT	42-78155/78314	160	B-24L-10-CO	44-41549/41648	100
B-24D-45-CO	42-40258/40322	65	B-246-15-NT	42-78315/78352	38	B-24L 15-CO	44-41649/41748	100
B-24D-50-CO	42-40323/40344	22	B-24G-16-NT	42-78353/78474	122	B-24L-20-CO	44-41749/41806	58
B-24D-53-CO	42-40345/40392	48	B-24J-2-NT	42-78475	1	B-24M-1-CO	44-41807/41848	42
B-24D-55-CO	42-40393/40432	40	B-24J-1-NT	42-78476/78794	319	B-24M-5-CO	44-41849/41948	100
B-24D-60-CO	42-40433/40482	50	B-24H-15-FO	42-94729/94794	66	B-24M-10-CO	44-41949/42048	100
B-24D-65-CO	42-40483/40527	45	B-24H-20-FO	42-94795/95022	228	B-24M-15-CO	44-42049/42148	100
B-24D-70-CO	42-40528/40567	40	B-24H-25-FO	42-95023/95288	226	B 24M-20-CO	44-42149/42248	100
B-24D-75-CO	42-40568/40612	45	B-24H-30-FO	42-95289/95503	215	B 24M-25-CO	44-42249/42348	100
B-24D-80-CO	42-40613/40652	40	B-24J-1-FO	42-95504/95628	125	B-24M-30-CO	44 42349/42448	100
B-24D-85-CO	42-40653/40697	45	B-24J-15-CF	42-99736/99805	70	B-24M-35-CO	44-42449/42548	100
B-24D-90-CO	42-40698/40742	45	B-24J-20-CF	42-99806/99871	66	B-24M-40-CO	44-42549/42648	100
B-24D-95-CO	42-40743/40787	45	B-24J-25-CF	42-99872/99935	64	B-24M-45-CO	44-42649/42722	74
B-24D-100-CO	42-40788/40822	35	B-24J-55-CO	42-99936/99985	50	B-24J-85-CF	44-44049/44148	100
B-24D-105-CO	42-40823/40867	45	B-24J-60-CO	42-99986/100035	50	B-24J-90-CF	44-44149/44248	100
B-24D-110-CO	42-40868/40917	50	B-24J-65-CO	42-100036/100085	50	B-24J-95-CF	44-44249/44348	100
B-24D-115-CO	42-40918/40962	45	B-24J-70-CO	42-100086/100135	50	B-24J-100-CF	44-44349/44448	100
B-24D-120-CO	42-40963/41002	40	B-24J-75-CO	42-100136/100185	50	B-24J-105-CF	44-44449/44501	53
B-24D-125-CO	42-41003/41047	45	B-24J-80-CO	42-100186/100235	50	XB-24N (FO)	44-48753	1
B-24D-130-CO	42-41048/41092	45	B-24J-85-CO	42-100236/100285	50	B-24J-20-FO	44-48754/49001	248
B-24D-135-CO	42-41093/41137	45	B-24J-90-CO	42-100286/100335	50	B-24L-1-FO	44-49002/49251	250
B-24D-140-CO	42-41138/41172	35	B-24J-95-CO	42-100336/100385	50	B 24L-5-FO	44-49252/49501	250
B-24D-145-CO	42-41173/41217	45	B-24J-100-CO	42-100386/100435	50	B-24L-10-FO	44-49502/49751	250
B-24D-150-CO	42-41218/41257	40	C-87 (CF)	42-107249/107265	17	B-24L-15-FO	44-49752/50001	250
B-24H-20-CF	42-50277/50354	78	AT-22 (CF)	42-107266	1	B 24L-20-FO	44-50002/50251	250
B-24H-25-CF	42-50355/50410	56	C-87 (CF)	42-107267/107275	9	B-24M-1-FO	44-50252/50451	200
B-24H-30-CF	42-50411/50451	41	B-24J-105-CO	42-109789/109838	50	B-24M-5-FO	44-50452/50651	200
B-24J-401-CF	42-50452/50508	57	B-24J-110-CO	42-109839/109888	50	B-24M-10-FO	44-50652/50851	200
B-24J-1-FO	42-50509/50759	251	B-24J-115-CO	42-109889/109938	50	B-24M-15-FO	44-50852/51051	200
B-24J-5-FO	42-50760/51076	317	B-24J-120-CO	42-109939/109988	50	B-24M-20-FO	44-51052/51251	200
B-24H-20-DT	42-51077/51103	27	B-24J-125-CO	42-109989/110038	50	B-24M-25-FO	44-51252/51451	200
B-24H-25-DT	42-51104/51181	73	B-24J-130-CO	42-110039/110088	50	B-24M-25-FO	44-51452/51928	477
B-24H-30-DT	42-51182/51225	44	B-24J-135-CO	42-110089/110138	50	YB-24N (FO)	44-52053/52059	7
B-24J-1-DT	42-51226/51292	67	B-24J-140-CO	42-110139/110188	50	C-87 (CF)	44-52978/52987	10
B-24J-5-DT	42-51293/51395	103	C-87 (CF)	43-30548	1			
B-24J-10-DT	42-51396/51430	35	AT-22 (CF)	43-30549	1			
B-24J-5-FO	42-51431/51610	180	C-87 (CF)	43-30550/30560	11			
B-24J-10-FO	42-51611/51825	215	AT-22 (CF)	43-30561	1			
B-24J-15-FO	42-51826/52075	250	C-87 (CF)	43-30562/30568	7			
B-24J-20-FO	42-52076	1	C-87A (CF)	43-30569/30571	3			
B-24H-5-FO	42-52077/52113	37	C-87 (CF)	43-30572/30573	2	Navy Cognisance Aircraft		
B24H-10-FO	42-52114/52302	189	AT-22 (CF)	43-30574	1	PB4Y-2 (CO)	59350/60009	660
B-24H-15-FO	42-52303/52776	474	C-87 (CF)	43-30575/30583	9	PB4Y-2 (CO)	66245/66324	80
B-24D-1-CF	42-63752/63796	45	AT-22 (CF)	43 30584	1	RY-3 (CO)	90020/90050	31
B-24D-5-CF	42-63797/63836	40	C-87 (CF)	43-30585/40627	43	RY3 (CO)	90057/90059	3

Appendix 3
B-24 Specifications

Model	B-24A	B-24D	B-24H/J	B-24M	C-87
Crew	8/10	8/10	8/10	8/10	5 & 25 passengers
Power Plant	4 x 1,200 hp R-1830-33	4 x 1,200 hp R-1830-43	4 x 1,200 hp R-1830-65	4 x 1,200 hp R-1830-65	4x1,200 hp R-1830-43
Wingspan	110 ft 0 in	110 ft 0 in	110 ft 0 in	110 ft 0 in	110 ft 0 in
Length	63 ft 9 in	66 ft 4 in	67 ft 2 in	67 ft 2 in	66 ft 4 in
Height	18 ft 8 in	17 ft 11 in	18 ft 0 in	18 ft 0 in	18 ft 0 in
Wing area	1,048 sq ft	1,048 sq ft	1,048 sq ft	1,048 sq ft	1,048 sq ft
Empty weight	30,000 lb	32,605 lb	36,500 lb	36,000 lb	31,935 lb
Max weight	53,600 lb	60,000 lb	65,000 lb	64,500 lb	56,000 lb
Max speed	292 mph/ 15,000 ft	303 mph / 25,000 ft	290 mph / 25,000 ft	300 mph/ 30,000 ft	306 mph
Cruising speed	228 mph	200 mph	215 mph	215 mph	–
Climb	5.6 mins/ 10,000 ft	22 mins/ 20,000 ft	25 mins/ 20,000 ft	25 mins/ 20,000 ft	20.9 mins/ 20,000 ft
Service ceiling	30,500 ft	32,000 ft	28,000 ft	28,000 ft	31,000 ft
Range	2,200 miles	2,850 miles	2,100 miles	2,100 miles	2,900 miles
Armament	6 x 0.50-in 2 x 030-in	10 x 0.50-in	10 x 0.50-in	10 x 0.50-in	1x 0.50-in
Bomb load	4,000 lb	8,800 lb	8,800 lb	8,800 lb	None

Appendix 4
Museum Aircraft and Survivors

A dozen complete Liberators survive, of which four are on static display in museums in the USA, and three are currently still flyable.

United States
B-24D-160-CO 42-72843 *Strawberry Bitch* is displayed at the Air Force Museum at Wright Patterson AFB, Dayton, Ohio. In World War 2 it served in the 512th BS, 376th 'Liberandos' BG, flying 59 missions. *Strawberry Bitch* spent thirteen years at Davis-Monthan AFB, Arizona, before being flown by Col Albert J. Shower, wartime CO of the 467th BG, 8th AF, to the Air Force Museum in 1959.

Ex-Indian Air Force B.VII (B-24J-90-CF 44-44175) (HE877/N7866) is on display at the Pima County Air Museum, Tucson, Arizona. Formerly liveried as 44-4175/HE877 *Paisano/Shoot You're Covered*, and later, *Red Ass* of the 446th BG at Bungay (Flixton), it has since been renamed *The Bungay Buckaroo*. B-24H-25-FO 42-95203 *Red Ass* was chosen by Col Jacob J. Brogger, CO, 446th BG 'Bungay Buckaroos' as his lead ship on D-Day 6 June 1944 when he was air commander, but public relations renamed the Liberator *The Buckaroo*!

At Castle AFB, California, is B-24M-5-CO/PB4Y-1 44-41916 / BuNo 90165, which is displayed as *Shady Lady*. This Liberator served in the 329th BS, 93rd BG in the 8th AF at Hardwick in WW2. B-24J-20-FO 44-48781 *Laden Maiden* is displayed at the Eighth Air Force Museum, Barkesdale AFB, LA.

Three airworthy Liberators exist in the USA. LB-30 AM927 (N12905) *Diamond Lil* is operated by the Commemorative (formerly Confederate) Air Force. No. 18 off the production lines, it is the oldest surviving B-24. AM927 was originally intended for 'special duties' with the RAF, but it suffered an accident on its delivery flight and was subsequently rebuilt by Consolidated. Converted to C-87 configuration, it operated as a company plane throughout the war. Flying a scheduled route between San Diego, Fort Worth and New York, the LB-30 became familiar as 'Old 927', from its original British serial number. Post-war it served with the Continental Can Company for ten years, then Petroleos Mexicanos, the Mexican national oil company. The CAF acquired 'Old 927' in 1967 and it now flies in the colours and markings of the 9th AF.

In June 1992 *Diamond Lil* flew the Atlantic once again, to Norwich, Norfolk, as part of the USAAF Fiftieth Anniversary celebrations in East Anglia. *Lil* took off from Fort Worth. Texas, and transited through Canada, Iceland and Prestwick, Scotland. Engine problems *en route* delayed *Diamond Lil*'s arrival in Britain and plagued her appearances and departure, which only went ahead in July after a replacement engine was airlifted to Biggin Hill.

B-24J-95-CF 44-44272/N94459, built by Consolidated at Fort Worth, was delivered to the RAF as a B.Mk.VI late in 1944. Later, it operated with No. 6 Squadron, Indian Air Force. In 1973 it was acquired by David Tallichet Jr., for 'Yesterday's Air Force' at Chino, California. N94459 was flown from Poona, India to the

USA but engine trouble meant it had to land at RAF Mildenhall, England. It was flown to Duxford for repair but remained at the famous Cambridgeshire airfield until August 1975, by which time it had received a new No. 3 engine and was fully restored. It was named *Delectable Doris*, in memory of 42-50551 *Delectable Doris* of the 566th BS, 389th BG at Hethel, Norfolk, which FTR with Lt Robert W. Bonnar's crew on 3 February 1945. On 25 August 1975 *Delectable Doris* was flown to Prestwick, where its nose-wheel collapsed on landing, and it only continued to the USA via Iceland after repairs costing £4,000. *Doris* was later purchased by Kermit Weeks, owner of the world's largest private aircraft collection; and later repainted as *Joe*, for an appearance in a TV movie about Joe Kennedy Jr. The B-24 has retained its 389th BG markings, and is now on display at Kermit Weeks's 'Fantasy of Flight' aviation theme park at Polk City, Florida.

B-24J-85-CF 44-44052 KH191, an ex-Indian Air Force B.VIII was at the IAF Technical College at Jalahalli, when in 1982 it was airfreighted to Great Britain for Warbirds of GB Ltd at Blackbushe. In 1986 KH191 was shipped to the USA and beautifully restored to airworthy condition by Tom Reilly of Kissimmee, Florida for the Collings Foundation of Stowe, Massachusetts. The B-24J was rebuilt in August 1989 as the *All American*. In recent years this Liberator has received the striking 'Dragon and his Tail' scheme once applied to B-24J-190-CO 44-40973 of the 64th BS, 43rd BG at Ie Shima in 1945.

India
The IAF Museum at Palam has retained B-24J-90-CF 44-44213.

Turkey
In spring 1972 an amateur diver found the wreck of B-24D-25-CO 41-24311 *Hadley's Harem*. It was a 98th BG veteran of the Ploesti raid, on 1 August 1943, which was ditched near Manavgat, Turkey, after losing two engines trying to reach Cyprus. It took 20 years for the cockpit section, which contained the remains of Lt James R. Lindsay, Capt Gilbert R. Hadley's co-pilot, to be raised. The forward fuselage section was restored and is on display at the Rahmi M. Koc museum in Istanbul, Turkey.

Canada
In Canada, at the National Aeronautical Collection at Trenton, Ontario, is B-24L-20-FO 44-50154 HE773, which is painted as 'RCAF 11130'. Among the current restoration projects worldwide is the rebuild by Tom Reilly Vintage Aircraft of a PB4Y-2 to fly using a B-24D fuselage.

Australia
The RAAF, which operated J/R and JR versions of the B-24, referred to the radar-equipped late models as B-24M/Rs, which post-war, (though the lightweight L was selected for some special duties) were used as a stop-gap bomber and maritime reconnaissance platform until the Australian-built Lincoln entered service. B-24M/R A72-176 (B-24M-10-CO 44-41956), one of only 47 M models delivered to the RAAF, is under restoration for static display. A72-176 served in 7 OTU at RAAF Tocumwal and post-war was modified for Antarctic operations (the nose turret and bomb-aimer's chin turret were removed and replaced with a clear panel). Grp Capt Deryk Kingwell used A72-176 as his personal aircraft while he was CO of Tocumwal and East Sale in 1946. The last flights A72-176 made were East Sale–Williamtown–East Sale on 22 March 1946 before becoming Instructional Airframe No. 5 at Crew Conversion Unit, East Sale. It was rescued from scrapping by George and James Toye, who removed the wings correctly, paid a 'couple of hundred pounds for it' and took the fuselage home to Moe in Victoria's La Trobe Valley. In 1988 the B-24 Liberator Memorial Restoration Fund Inc. obtained the aircraft and it is presently in a hangar at Werribee near Melbourne nearing completion. A large amount of money was

paid for the wing of AL557 (N92MK), which had crash-landed at Anchorage in 1958. In 1991 another wing was discovered on B-24D-130-CO 42-41091 *Bunny Hop*, 403rd BS, 43rd BG, which made an emergency landing on the Faita emergency strip in the Ramu Valley south of Madang after damage from a fighter attack during an armed reconnaissance of the Wewak area. The fuselage had been cut up for scrap but never collected. The undercarriage was damaged in the landing and the aircraft abandoned. This wing was removed and transported to Australia. Restoration of the wing is almost complete and it has been attached to the fuselage of A72-176. As well as items purchased from the US, pieces from *Poochie*, lying on the delta of the Daly River in the Northern Territory, B24D-53-CO 42-40387 *Beautiful Betsy*, and B-24D 42-41091 *Dis-Gusted*, recovered from Long Field in the Northern Territory, have been used. A72-176 should be completely restored by 2004. Further funds are being raised to house the aircraft on display.

United Kingdom
The 'Cosford Liberator' is an ex-RAF/IAF Liberator, built as a B-24L-20-FO (44-50206) and delivered to 99 Squadron RAF on 26 June 1945. It served on detachment in the Cocos Islands where the Squadron CO and the SAAF Station Commander flew it. No. 99 Squadron disbanded in November 1945 and the Liberator was finally struck off charge on 11 April 1946 at No. 322 MU, Cawnpore. It was later refurbished by Hindustan Aeronautics to serve with No. 6 Squadron, RIAF at Poona. As HE807 it remained in service until 31 December 1968, when it was placed in open storage at Bangalore. Six years later it was presented to the RAF Museum, arriving at RAF Lyneham on 7 July 1974, and was then sent to RAP Colerne. When Colerne closed, the Liberator had its wings cut off before being transported by road to its present location at The Aerospace Museum Cosford, at Shifnal, Shropshire, where it is on static display with its wings reattached.

The American Air Museum at Duxford has two Liberator exhibits. It acquired from the National Air and Space Museum in Washington DC, a nose assembly from a B-24D, and the forward fuselage of B-24J-5-FO 42-51457. These have been used to create a nose exhibit to represent B-24D-90-CO 42-40738, *Fightin' Sam*, with the squadron insignia of the 566th BS, 389th BG when it became the ship commanded by Maj Tom Conroy, the squadron CO. The most recent Liberator addition is EZB-24M-20-FO 44-51228, which was previously on display at Lackland AFB, San Antonio, Texas, before being acquired by the IWM early in 2001. It became the last Liberator to be used by the USAF, when in 1953–4 it was used for ice-research tests. Completely restored to represent B-24M-5-FO 44-50493 *Dugan*, which flew in the 578th BS, 392nd BG at Wendling, Norfolk in 1945, it took its rightful place in the American Air Museum in June 2002.

'Dugan' was the nickname given to the father of Col Robert (Bob) Vickers, a pilot in the 392nd BG, by an Irish friend. The Vickers family has no Irish connections but the nickname was used as a term of endearment. 44-51228 is similar to 44-50493 but the former, which differs in having a V-shape windshield, was not assigned to operational groups before the war ended. *Dugan's* scheme sported a four-leaf clover on both sides of its nose and the engine cowlings were painted red. 44-50493, which arrived at Wendling on 8 February 1945, was assigned to Vickers' crew after they had been forced to abandon 42-51121 *Niagara Special* over the Continent on their second mission on 16 January 1945. *Dugan* went on to fly 28 combat missions in the 392nd BG and Col Vickers finished the war with 30 missions, 26 of which were as pilot of *Dugan*, and 20 of those with his own crew. On the other six missions he flew as Command Pilot with other crews. Vickers, an American Air Museum Founding Member and Board member, as well as a long time friend of Duxford flew *Dugan* on two Berlin missions and on five trips to Magdeburg's notorious oil refineries.

Appendix 5
B-24 Units 1944–5

8th Air Force, England, 1944–5
2nd Air Division
2nd Combat Bomb Wing
389th Bomb Group (564th, 565th, 566th, 567th Bomb Squadrons)
445th BG (700th, 701st, 702nd, 703rd BS)
453rd BG (732nd, 733rd, 734th, 735th BS)
14th Combat Bomb Wing
44th BG (66th, 67th, 68th, 506th BS)
392nd BG (576th, 577th, 578th, 579th BS)
492nd BG (856th, 857th, 858th, 859th BS)
      withdrawn from combat, 7 August 1944.
      Replaced by 491st BG 14 August 1944
20th Combat Bomb Wing
93rd BG (328th, 329th, 330th, 409th BS)
446th BG (704th, 705th, 706th, 707th BS)
448th BG 712th, 713th, 714th, 715th BS)
95th Combat Bomb Wing
489th BG (844th, 845th, 846th, 847th BS)
      to 20th CBW, Non-op 14 November 1944
491st BG (852nd, 853rd, 854th, 855th BS)
      to 14th CBW 14 August 1944

3rd Bomb Division
93rd Combat Bomb Wing
490th BG (848th, 849th, 850th, 851st BS)
493rd BG (860th, 861st, 862nd, 863rd BS)
      Wing converted to B-17G August–September 1944
92nd CBW/4th Combat Bomb Wing (P)
34th BG (4th, 7th, 18th, 391st BS)
486th BG (832nd, 833rd, 834th, 835th BS)
487th BG (836th, 837th, 838th, 839th BS)
      Wing converted to B-17G August–September 1944)

15th Air Force, Italy, January 1944–5
47th Bomb Wing
98th BG (343rd, 344th, 345th, 415th BS)
376th BG (512th, 513th, 514th, 515th BS)
449th BG (716th, 717th, 718th, 719th BS)
450th BG (720th, 721st, 722nd, 723rd BS)
49th Bomb Wing
451st BG (724th, 725th BS, 726th, 727th BS)
461st BG (764th, 755th BS, 766th, 767th BS)
484th BG (824th, 825th BS, 826th, 827th BS)
55th Bomb Wing
460th BG (760th, 761st BS, 767th, 768th BS)
464th BG (776th, 777th BS, 778th, 779th BS)
465th BG (780th, 781st BS, 782nd, 783rd BS)
485th BG (828th, 829th BS, 830th, 831st BS)
304th Bomb Wing
454th BG (736th, 737th, 738th, 739th BS)
455th BG (740th, 741st BS, 742nd, 743rd BS)
456th BG (744th, 745th BS, 746th, 747th BS)
459th BG (755th, 757th BS, 758th, 759th BS)
2641st (Special) Group (Provisional)
885th BS (H) From July 1944
859th BS (H) From January 1945

USN PB4Y-1 Squadrons
Atlantic
VP-103 (Operational from March 1943); VP-105 (May 1943); VP-107 (June 1943); VP-110 (October 1943); VP-111 (October 1943); VP-112 (October 1943); VP-113 (October 1943); VP-114 (November 1943); VPB-125 (February–March 1944); VPB-163 (December 1943–January 1944)

Pacific
Photo-Reconnaissance: VD-1 (January 1943); VD-3 (February 1943); VD-4 (August 1943); VD-5 (July–August 1943)
Patrol: VB-101 (October 1942); VB-102 (October 1943); VB-104 (May 1943); VB-106 (June 1943); VB-108 (June 1943); VB-109 (September 1943); VB-115 (December 1943); VB-116 (January 1944); VB-117 (October1944); VPB-118 (January 1945); VPB-200 (May 1944 – 1st sqdn to receive PB4Y-2)

Aleutians, Alaska
11th Air Force
28th Composite Group
36th BS (and B-17s), 21st BS 404th BS

CBI (China–Burma–India) theatre
10th Air Force
7th BG, Strategic AF (9th, 436th, 492nd, 483rd BS)
Eastern Air Command
24th Combat Mapping Squadron, 8th Photo Recce Group
14th Air Force (India–Burma)
308th BG+ (373rd, 374th, 375th, 425th BS) B-24 and C-87
RAF (SEAC) (India)
357 (Special Duties), 150, 200, 354, 355, 159 Squadrons, 99 and 355 Squadrons in Cocos Islands

Pacific Air Forces
5th Air Force (SW Pacific)
22nd BG (2nd, 19th, 33rd, 408th BS)
43rd BG (63rd, 64th, 65th, 403rd BS)
90th BG (319th, 320th, 321st, 400th BS)
380th BG (328th, 329th, 330th, 331st BS)
20th Combat Mapping Squadron
7th Air Force (Central Pacific)
11th BG (14th, 26th, 42nd, 98th, 431st BS)
30th BG (21st, 27th, 38th, 392nd, 819th BS)
494th BG (864th, 865th, 866th, 867th BS)
86th Combat Mapping Squadron
20th Air Force
3rd Photo-Recce Squadron
655th BS (55th Weather Recce Squadron)
13th Air Force (China–West Pacific)
5th BG (23rd, 31st, 72nd, 394th BS)
307th BG (370th, 371st, 372nd, 424th BS)

RAAF (Australia)
21, 23, 24, 25 Squadrons

RAF Air Command South-East Asia 1 July 1944
222 Group, 160 Squadron; 225 Group, 200, 354 Squadrons; 231 Group, 175 Wing, 99 Squadron; 184 Wing, 355, 356 Squadrons; 185 Wing, 159 Squadron;
No. 357 (Special Duties) Squadron

RAF Coastal Command
53, 59, 86, 120, 200, 206, 220, 224, 233, 301, 502, 547 Squadrons

Mediterranean
Allied Strategic Air Force, Italy
No. 205 Group (37, 40, 70, 104, 178 Squadrons)

Balkan Air Force SOE (Special Operations Executive)
148, 301 (Pomeranian–Polish), 624 Squadrons

SAAF
2 Wing SAAF (31, 34 Squadrons)

Appendix 6
Model Kits

Part No.	Item	Maker	Scale
MODEL KITS – INTERNATIONAL BRANDS			
AC1692	B-24D Liberator	ACADEMY	1:72
AC1693	B-24H Liberator	ACADEMY	1:72
AC1694	B-24J Liberator	ACADEMY	1:72
AC2135	B-24D Nose Art	ACADEMY	1:72
AC2152	B-24M Liberator	ACADEMY	1:72
AC2160	B-24H Liberator *Aries*	ACADEMY	1:72
AC2163	B-24H Lib. *Zodiac Aquarius*	ACADEMY	1:72
AC2168	B-24H *Zodiac* nose art	ACADEMY	1:72
AC2172	B-24H Liberator *Zodiac Leo*	ACADEMY	1:72
AX06010	B-24J Liberator	AIRFIX	1:72
ID32B3	B-24J Liberator	ID MODELS	1:32
Vac Form			
MC11612	B-24D Liberator *The Goon*	MINICRAFT	1:72
MC11614	B-24J Liberator *Dragon and his Tail*	MINICRAFT	1:72
MC14402	B-24J Liberator	MINICRAFT	1:144
MG560	B-24D Liberator	MONOGRAM	1:48
MG5608	B-24J Liberator	MONOGRAM	1:48
MG5932	B-24D Liberator with interior	MONOGRAM	1:48
RV433924	B-24D Liberator	REVELL	1:72
RV4339L	B-24D Liberator	REVELL	1:72
DETAILING ACCESSORIES			
Resin and Photo etched			
AEC72179	B-24 Liberator	AIRWAVES	1:72
ED72065	B-24D Liberator	EDUARD	1:72
ED72066	B-24J Liberator	EDUARD	1:72
ED72191	B-24J Liberator	EDUARD	1:72
ED72193	B-24 bomb bay	EDUARD	1:72
EDXF118	B-24J Liberator	EDUARD	1:48
EDXS138	B-24D Liberator	EDUARD	1:72
FHP48014	B-24J Liberator Detail Set	FLIGHTPATH	1:48
PAR48093	RAF 100 Group B-17G & B-24J/M	PARAGON DESIGNS	1:48
PAR72042	RAF 100 Group B-17G & B-24J/M	PARAGON DESIGNS	1:72
SQS9141	B-24H/J Cockpit canopy	SQUADRON	1:72
SQS9142	B-24H/J Ball turret	SQUADRON	1:72
SQS9143	B-24D Cockpit canopy	SQUADRON	1:72
SQS9571	B-24J Liberator Main	SQUADRON	1:48
SQS9573	B-24H/J Liberator	SQUADRON	1:48
SQS9588	B-24D nose and main x 1	SQUADRON	1:48
TD41305	B-24D Liberator	TRUE DETAILS FAST	1:48
TD48024	B-24A/M	TRUE DETAILS	1:48
TD48475	B-24 Liberator	TRUE DETAILS	1:48
TD72016	B-24 Liberator/PB4Y-2	TRUE DETAILS	1:72

Part No.	Item	Maker	Scale
DECALS			
AMD72019	B-24 Liberator Collection	AEROMASTER	1:72
AMD72020	B-24 Liberators Galore	AEROMASTER	1:72
AMD72113	B-24J Liberator over Europe Pt 1	AEROMASTER	1:72
AMD72114	B-24 Liberator over Europe Pt 2	AEROMASTER	1:72
SS48031	B-24J 392BG; 458BG; 406BS	SUPERSCALE	1:48
SS48032	B-24J 90BG 5AF; 491BG	SUPERSCALE	1:48
SS48037	B-24J *Dragon and his Tail*	SUPERSCALE	1:48
SS48265	B-24D Goon; Ripper the 1	SUPERSCALE	1:48
SS48340	B-24D & J Liberators. Flak Alley	SUPERSCALE	1:48
SS48484	B-24 Liberator	SUPERSCALE	1:48
SS48485	B-24J Liberator	SUPERSCALE	1:48
SS48625	B-24D	SUPERSCALE	1:48
SS48626	B-24D	SUPERSCALE	1:48
SS72024	Famous B-24D/J Liberators	SUPERSCALE	1:72
SS72163	B-24J (6) 445/308BG; 64/759/7	SUPERSCALE	1:72
SS72280	US Army (4) A-20B B-24D B-25C	SUPERSCALE	1:72
SS72281	Bomb Groups. B-17 386th, B-24	SUPERSCALE	1:72
SS72476	B-24J (4) 90BG; 491BG *Tubarão*;	SUPERSCALE	1:72
SS72499	B-24J (3) All 43BG Pacific	SUPERSCALE	1:72
SS72574	B-24D/J (3) D 68BS; J 579BS;	SUPERSCALE	1:72
SS72683	B-24J Liberator	SUPERSCALE	1:72
SS72684	B-24J Liberator	SUPERSCALE	1:72
SS72750	B-24D Ploesti Raid	SUPERSCALE	1:72
SS72751	B-24D	SUPERSCALE	1:72
SS72752	B-24D	SUPERSCALE	1:72
SS72753	B-24J/M	SUPERSCALE	1:72
SS72783	B-24J Liberators	SUPERSCALE	1:72
VA4878	Australian B-24M *Penelope II*	VENTURA DECALS	1:48
VA7267	Australian B-24M *Penelope II*	VENTURA DECALS	1:72
VA7268	SEAC B-24	VENTURA DECALS	1:72
X02172	B-17 & B-24 in RAF Service	XTRADECALS	1:72
X02572	B-24H Liberator 8th AF	XTRADECALS	1:72

Information provided by Hannants
Tel 00 44 (0)1502 517444 (8 lines)
Fax: 00 44 (0)1502 500521
Email: david@hannants.co.uk
Web Site: http://www.hannants.co.uk
Postal Address: H. G. Hannant Ltd, Harbour Road, Oulton
Broad, Lowestoft, Suffolk, NR32 3LZ, England

Appendix 7
Liberator Books

A Bomber Pilot in WWII – From Farm Boy to Pilot: 35 Missions in the B-24 Walter F. Hughes, Fremont, CA
A Missing Plane Susan Sheehan
Ad Lib: Flying the B-24 Liberator in WWII William Carigan, Sunflower University Press, Manhattan, KS, 1988
Against All Odds Major Frederick D. Worthen (Ret), Fithian Press
American Combat Planes Ray Wagner, Doubleday & Co, Garden City, NY, 1982
Aphrodite: Desperate Mission Jack Olsen, G. P. Putnam's sons, New York, NY,1970
Attack – Death in the Skies Over the Middle East Richard G. Byers
Attlebridge Diaries, Lt-Col John H. Woolnough, Newsphoto Yearbooks, San Angelo, TX, l979
Bail Out Mel TenHaken
Booster McKeester & other Experiences 98th BG Middle East Theater 1942–43 Willie Chapman, Long Beach, CA
B-24 Liberator Units of the Pacific War Robert F. Dorr, Osprey Publishing Ltd, England 1999
B-24 Liberator Units of the 8th Air Force Robert F. Dorr, Osprey, 2000
B-24 Liberator Units of the Fifteenth Air Force Robert F. Dorr, Osprey, 2001
B-24 Liberator Frederick A. Johnson, Motorbooks, Osceola, WI, 1993
B-24 Liberator at War Roger Freeman, Motorbooks, Osceola, WI, 1983
B-24 Liberator in Action Squadron Signal Publications, Carrollton, TX, 1987
B-24 Nose Art Name Directory Wallace Foreman, Specialty Press, North Branch, MN
Boots From Heaven Janet L. Howard and Odile Lavandier
Camouflage & Markings B-24 Liberator Ducimus Books Ltd, Staples Printers, London
Carpetbaggers Ben Parnell, Eakin Press, Austin, TX, 1987
Coffee Tower A History of the 459th BG in WWII Lyle H. McCarty, privately printed, 1987
Consolidated B-24 Liberator John M. & Donna Campbell, Schiffer Publishing Ltd, Atglen, PA, 1993
Consolidated B-24 Liberator Early Models Philip J. R. Moyes, Visual Art Press, Oxford, England, 1979
Consolidated B-24D-M Liberator Ernest R McDowell, Arco Publishing Co, NY, 1969
Cuckoo Over Vienna Claude L. Porter, Village Press Inc., Traverse City, MI, 1989
Descending To Go Above and Beyond Donna DiMasicio, Squadron Publishers, Rensselaer, NY
Eagle of the Pacific Edwin & Jeanne L. Spight, Historical Aviation Album, Temple City, CA, 1980
Eight Bailed Out Maj James M. Inks, Popular Library, Eagle Books, NY, 1954
ETO Carpetbaggers George A. Reynolds
Famous Bombers of Second World War William Green, Doubleday & Co, Garden City, NY, 1959
Fields of Little America Martin W. Bowman, Patrick Stephens Ltd, Cambridge, England, 1977
Flight Manual for B-24 Liberator USAAC Aviation Publications, Appleton, WI, 1977
General Dynamics Aircraft and Predecessors John Wegg, Naval Institute Press, Annapolis, MD, 1990
General Service Notes Model 32 (B-24) Consolidated Aircraft Corp., 1942
Jaws Over Europe Ursel P. Harvel, privately printed, Ursel P. Harvel, Ellington, FL
Lady Be Good Dennis E. McClendon, Aero Publishers Inc., Fallbrook, CA, 1982
Liberator John McSweeny, General Dynamics
Liberator Lore Vols. 1 to 4 Frederick A. Johnson, Frederick A. Johnson Publisher, Tacoma, WA, 1989

Liberator Pilot: The Cottontails' Battle for Oil Vincent F. Fagan, California Aero Press, Carlsbad, CA, 1991
Log of the Liberators Steve Birdsall, Doubleday & Co., Garden City, NY, 1973
Low Level Mission Leon Wolf, Berkley Publishing Corp., New York, NY, 1957
Low Level Liberators The Story of Patrol Bombing Squadron 104 in the South Pacific during WWII Paul Stevens, Nashville, TN
Lucky B-24 Arthur Anthony, privately published
Maternity Ward: Final Flight of a WWII Liberator Margueritte Madison Aronowitz, Pine Castle Books, Prescott, AZ
Marking & Camouflage 1941–45 B-24 Liberator E. A. Munday, Osprey
Missions of Shehasta: A Story of WWII Bomber Aces Lyman A. Clark Jr., Fairmont, WV
MIA – World War Two F. N. Kautzmann, Austin Press, Delaware, OH
Mission Failure and Survival Charles McBride
Pilot Training Manual B-24 Liberator HQ, AAF Office of Flying Safety, AAF Office of Flying Safety, 1944
Ploesti Oil Strike John Sweetman, Ballantine Books, New York, NY, 1974
Ploesti. The Great Ground Air Battle of 1 August 1943 James Dugan & Carroll Stewart, Fletcher & Son, 1963
Red Roses and Silver Wings. A WWII Memoir Kitty Strickland Shore, Twiggs Company, Rapid City, SD
Replacement Crew Richard C. Baynes, Irvine, CA
Rider On The Wind David Westheimer (fiction)
Secret Squadrons of the Eighth Pat Carty, Speciality Press, Stillwater MN, 1990
Slacks and Calluses. Our Summer in a Bomber Factory Constance Bowman/Clara Marie Allen, 1944
Sporty Course: Memoirs of a World War II Bomber Pilot Jack Swayze
Stranger In Their Land CBI Bombardier 1939–1945 Thurzal Q. Terry
Tales of a Tail Gunner Eddie Picardo, Hara Publishing, Seattle, WA
Target Ploesti Leroy W. Newby, Presidio Press, Novato, CA, 1983
Ten Knights in a Bar Room: Missing in Action in the South Pacific 1943 Michael J. Cundiff, Books on Demand, 1990
The Bedford Triangle Martin W. Bowman, PSL, 1988, Sutton Publishing, 1996
The B-24 Liberator Allen G. Blue, Charles Scribners & Sons, NY
The B-24 Liberator Steve Birdsall, Doubleday Publishing Co., NY, 1979
The B-24 Liberator 1939–1945 Martin W. Bowman, Rand McNally, NY, 1980
The B-24J Liberator Roger A. Freeman, Profile Publications, Leatherhead, England, 1965
The Bomber Barons Frederick A. Johnson, Bomber Books, Tacoma, WA, 1982
The Desert Rats Michael Hill, Pictorial Histories Publishing Co., Missoula, MT, 1990
The Final Flight of Maggie's Drawers Ray E. Zinck, Turner Publishing, Paducah, KY
The Fortunes of War Allan G. Blue, Aero Publishers, Inc., Fallbrook, CA, 1967
The 465th Remembered Book I & II Compiled by Gene F. Moxley, Warrenton, MO
The 446th Revisited 446th BG Assn., Santa Ana, CA
The Last Liberator (Novel) Jerry Yulsman
The War of the Cotton Tails William R. Cubbins, Algonquin Books, Chapel Hill, NC, 1989
Toward Sanctuary Bill Barnes, privately printed, 1945
United States Military Aircraft since 1909 F. G. Swanborough, Putnam, London, NY, 1963
US Bombers 1928 to 1980 Lloyd S. Jones, Aero Publishers Inc., Fallbrook, CA, 1980
Waist Gunner S. Sidney Ulmer, Xlibris, Philadelphia, PA
Wings Sentry Magazine, Sentry Books Inc., Granada Hills, CA, 1991

Index

Page numbers in *italics* refer to illustrations.